ACT ALIVE

The Essential Guide to Igniting and Sustaining Your Working Actor Career

Andi Matheny

Published by St. Petersburg Press
St. Petersburg, FL
www.stpetersburgpress.com

Design and composition by Isa Crosta and St. Petersburg Press
Cover design by Marc Brugnoni
Back cover photo by Leslie Hassler

Print ISBN: 978-1-940300-56-6
Ebook ISBN: 978-1-940300-57-3

First Edition

Dedicated to my beloved family of students.
You may have thought I was your teacher,
but the truth is,
you taught me everything.

Contents

PROLOGUE

THE ACTOR'S JOURNEY

It's never too late—never too late to start over,
never too late to be happy.
—Jane Fonda

Every time I try to tell the story of my life as an actor and acting coach, it strikes me how nonlinear and uhhh, *odd*, my journey has been. And then, in one of my many forehead-smacking moments, I said to myself, "Well of course your life has been odd, Andi. You're an *actor*!"

If you're reading this book, chances are you're odd too. You're likely one or all of these: misunderstood, artistic, sensitive, intelligent, struggling, unmentored, passionate, underestimated, a black sheep, child of alcoholics or other -oholics, nonconformist, overachiever, deep thinker who desperately wants to be an actor. Did I nail it? Yes? Then welcome to our wonderful, odd tribe. You can now cross off "unmentored" because you're reading the book I desperately needed when I first began my career and will hopefully be your go-to guide as a working actor from this day forward.

Here's the brief overview of my life BCA (before coaching actors): I graduated with a bachelor's in theater arts from UCLA with a lot of intellectual "college knowledge," but none of it translated to becoming a working actor in the real world. Oh, the frustration! I knew what good acting was; after all I worshipped Meryl Streep, Marlon Brando, and all of the other brilliant actors I grew up watching, but as soon as I picked up a script, I felt like I was made out of lead. One of my first agents said, "You really should try something else," right before they dropped me. I stunk so badly at auditions it's a wonder I wasn't chased out of Hollywood by casting directors carrying torches and mocha lattes.

After booking a couple of forgettable TV walk-ons, I quit and became a talk show host for a decade. Seriously. I had four nationally televised shows, almost all before the internet and Wikipedia. Told you I was odd! I married a screenwriter and transitioned back into acting, this time with a better agent and booking better roles, but none was all that satisfying. Anyone remember my tour de force as Jenny the nudist on *Monk*? I didn't think so. I was lucky to be a working actor, but I felt like something was missing.

Then the greatest thing happened. After losing almost everything during the 2008 financial crisis, we sold our house in Los Angeles and moved to St. Petersburg, Florida, for no other reason besides cheap real estate. I randomly decided to open an acting studio in this quirky town known more for its craft breweries than for its actors. That's when my life really began. My first class had ten students, most of whom had never laid eyes on a script before. Because most of these wonderful people had no clue about even the most basic of acting concepts, I had to get creative to communicate the essence of organic acting in what I called my "Annie Sullivan" moments. (Please don't make me explain who Annie Sullivan is. If you don't know, look her up.) Here's the story of my first major teaching epiphany, which transformed my life and the lives of my students, and was the seed that begat this book.

Several years ago, I had a student whom I'll call Rick (and for the rest of the book, almost all students' names have been changed). Rick was in his early twenties, had some modeling experience, but had never taken an acting class before in his life. When he was on stage performing a scene, he had a perpetually frozen, embarrassed smile on his face and was constantly sneaking peeks out at the audience to gauge their reaction to him. No matter how many notes I gave him, his performance didn't improve after weeks in class.

My actors choose their own scenes. I've found that actors have a genius for selecting material that they know will best help them, at least on a subconscious level. Rick brought in a scene from *Good Will Hunting*, about the emotionally scarred young math prodigy who at first has a contentious relationship with his therapist. The scene was the confrontational climax between the two men.

I noticed a little less of the frozen smile in this scene and a little more of a glimmer of a connection in Rick. We stopped the scene, and I asked Rick if he felt this scene was similar to other contentious relationships in his life.

His eyes welled with tears, and I realized we were on to something. He revealed that his father had abandoned him at an early age and that he had spent his life squelching the pain. On the spot, I had him improvise what he would say to his father if he were to show up today.

And then it was like watching Rick come alive. His stiffness melted away, his face had color, his eyes were on fire, and he wasn't worried about his "lines"—all he cared about was confronting his father. When he was finished, the class was stunned, as if we had all witnessed the same miracle. Where had this guy been all these weeks?

When he went back to the actual script of the scene, it was like watching a completely different human being. He used this newly established emotional *connection* to merge with the character he was portraying, and the result was riveting. But the amazing thing was, every scene he tackled thereafter was completely transformed as well. Rick had experienced unbridled freedom on stage, using the truthful experience from his own life and now understood to merge that feeling of freedom and connection with every *scripted* scene moving forward. This happened a while ago, but to this day, the students who witnessed Rick undergo such a seismic shift in one class still talk about it.

That was life-changing, not only for my teaching practice but my awareness as a former floundering actor. I remembered how desperately I would grasp for something outside of myself, how I was always trying to figure out how to "say lines" and how stiff and disconnected I usually felt. What we all saw watching Rick was that when he connected to his truth, his acting was effortless. The result was absolutely riveting.

It's not enough to have intellectual knowledge of acting. As I found out early on, that's no guarantee of a good performance. Because we're recreating human behavior, actors need to learn the craft on a physical, emotional, and spiritual level—or what I call "getting it into our bones." After the Rick Epiphany, whenever a student was struggling with a scene, I would create an exercise on the spot that quickly got them out of their head and into a visceral, spontaneous connection that would resonate on that "bone" level. Sometimes these exercises addressed major acting concepts, like substitution or character objective. Other times they focused on frequently occurring moments: memory moments or moments of recall, moments of rage and desperate need, moments of command and persuasion, or everyday moments that simply require ordinary human behavior. Time and again, we witnessed the lightbulb go off and a brilliant performance materialize like magic in our little St. Petersburg studio. All of those lightbulbs resulted in the exercises contained in these pages, and I believe they're the best and quickest way for any new actor to fully understand the organic nature of TV and film acting.

I realize some of the concepts and themes of this book have been around for a long time, much longer than I've been teaching. What I believe sets my approach apart is I have made them into tangible exercises that an actor can practice, like a dancer does barre exercises or a musician does scales. This approach is also a way of cutting to the chase—rather than sitting around talking about what you should be feeling or experiencing in any given moment, you experience it on the spot. As a result, when you start doing scenes, the process of scene work is accelerated because these exercises teach you to identify certain types of elements of a scene and compel you to get to the truth of a moment quickly.

There is a practical application in the real world as well. When you audition for film and TV, you may have less than twenty-four hours to master a multipage role. We actors don't have the luxury of wallowing in process—we need to get immediately connected to bring the character to life. The more disciplined you are to work this way, the better your chances are of giving a memorable audition and booking the role.

Remember when I said this is when my life began? As an acting teacher, I had a front-row seat watching lives change in miraculous ways. I saw my students, many of whom had been unhappily struggling with dead-end jobs prior to joining my studio, get their first agents and book their first movie and TV roles. I saw shy wallflowers blossom into confident, dynamic human beings. And between you and me—the discoveries I made while teaching new actors raised my own game as a working actor. I've worked more consistently in the past few years, booking the juiciest roles of my career. All this from the girl who was told she should try something else. Well, I did. I wrote a book. I'm convinced the discoveries that changed my life and the lives of others will now change yours, you beautiful odd person. Did that get your attention?

Good. Now let's get going.

HOW TO USE THIS BOOK

You already know how to act. You just don't trust it yet. The delightful discovery you will make with each chapter in this book is you already possess the raw material you need to be brilliant. Your experiences, your triumphs, your failures, your loves, your losses. The life you've lived up to this point is your gift as an actor, your secret weapon. You just need to learn how to channel these gifts and dive into the process of using them with an open mind and heart. As Glinda the Good Witch said in *The Wizard of Oz*, "You've always had the power." So you see, I'm not really teaching you anything. I'm just reminding you of what you already know.

I wanted this book to be as close to a classroom experience as possible, and reflect the journey you might take in my studio. Each chapter highlights an acting concept or a key lesson, and the corresponding exercises will build your acting muscle, like any athlete or artist undergoes conditioning before they compete or perform. As you read the book, you will notice how you will be able to recognize these concepts as separate tools, but at the same time how they all relate to each other, just like separate notes on a piano come together to play a song.

The exercises either encourage you to make observations (an ongoing journal is strongly suggested), write your own material (don't worry, it's easier than you think), or improvise (including dancing!). Some have script excerpts that help you digest the lesson. Start with the given text, but if you find yourself struggling, find your own. As you read the book, I encourage you to also read scripted material from the multiple resources on the web—movies, plays, and TV shows, both dramatic and comedic—and apply the concepts from each chapter as if you were preparing for a role in that project. The more scenes you work on, the better sense you'll have of script analysis and which exercises give you the key to unlock those scenes. If it's a script you're already familiar with, it'll give you a greater appreciation of how the actor achieved their results and will inspire you to create your own distinctive performances.

I encourage the new actor to try these exercises with a group of other dedicated actors. You can even do several of the exercises on your own. Remember to enjoy the process! The art of acting is a lifetime endeavor. Even our greatest actors feel like they've never quite mastered this craft. So, for those of you who have been at this for a while, maybe some of these exercises will inspire you to approach a script or an audition in a fresh way.

There are certain exercises that I have suggested you record yourself with a smartphone or other device. Do that as much as possible and get over the "But I hate looking at myself" excuse now. When you watch it back, make notes of what worked and what needs refining or even reworking. Become your own director and steward of your art. This will accelerate your progress, and the sooner you start, the faster you'll achieve mastery of your skills.

By the way, some acting classes or methods demand that you follow their protocol exactly as taught. Some have a checklist that you must adhere to or specific steps that you must follow in a certain order, and if you do not, you will fail to deliver your best work as an actor.

Act ALIVE is not designed with that kind of rigidity in mind. This isn't a cult—it's acting—and you, as the artist, have the freedom to use this approach as best serves you. Maybe one exercise alone is the key that unlocks a scene, for example using your Hot Person Confrontation (Part One). Or other exercises will lead you to a path of discovery and imagination that is exciting for a character you're playing. Some may not resonate with you at all. At the end of the day, the goal is to make this work for you, so that you can be a working actor. On a set, nobody cares about your "method." They want a pro who shows up on time, is pleasant to work with, and can deliver a believable performance.

If you're the type of actor who likes to soak up as much information as possible to improve your craft and get an edge on auditions, reading this book cover-to-cover starting at page 1 will open the doors to audition mastery that might have taken you years in a weekly acting class. But if you're saying to yourself, "That's a lot of chapters, and I have an audition tomorrow!"—I've organized the material into easily digestible sections that will best help you according to what your immediate needs are. No matter how you choose to read it, you'll find valuable nuggets to use now or file away for the future.

Part One — The Essential Actor. Whether you're a new or experienced actor, I encourage everyone to start here. This section gives you powerful tools for the majority of your auditions and scene work, for material ranging from simple and naturalistic to emotionally challenging. These exercises will get you on your feet quickly and will prepare you for a professional level of acting and auditioning within a relatively short period of time. I've also included an introduction to the subject of tone, which is continued in depth in Part Three and is essential knowledge for every actor, especially if your focus is TV and film.

Part Two — The Passionate Actor takes you on a deeper dive into ways to emotionally connect to the human being you're portraying in a script. If you have booked a lead on stage or screen or are preparing a meaty smaller role, these exercises help you find the truth in every moment of your character's life. When you perform these exercises, you will also notice they start to build an emotional and physical muscle memory. After a while, when a script calls for a specific type of moment, you won't necessarily need to do the exercise beforehand; you will just remember the muscle memory the exercise created and be instantly connected. Have fun digging in!

Part Three — The Pragmatic Actor introduces you to exercises that emphasize finding character through physicality and other techniques, including improvisation. This is the section that will help you nail those roles that don't necessarily demand an emotional connection and contains more "outside-in" methods to truthful performances. If you have a costar audition for a professional-type tomorrow, you need to read these chapters now.

Part Four — The Working Actor weaves the previous sections together and gives you more guidance on how to apply all of the concepts to scene work with script analysis and rehearsal tips. I have also included more anecdotes from class, which will illustrate how specific exercises dramatically transformed a scene.

Most of the scenes and scripts from TV and film referred to in this book are available online in more complete formats. I have links for them and other supplemental material for this book available at my website, www.andimathenyactingstudios.com. Or if you're a rugged individualist, you can do your own web surfing. Research is part of the actor's job, so get used to it now!

KEY TERMS

Andi's editor: In most books, glossaries are typically presented in alphabetical order.
Andi: Yeah, but this isn't most books.

If you haven't already skipped ahead, I wanted to give you a mini-glossary of terms that will be helpful when you read this book. You'll hear these terms over and over again, not only in this book but from other actors, casting directors, and movie and TV directors for the remainder of your acting career. You would probably glean what these terms mean while reading, but I will attempt to define them so we're on the same page going forward.

CONNECTED — When an actor understands on a visceral level how the character behaves, thinks, feels, and speaks—that is feeling *connected*. Sometimes this connection is so seamless that the lines are blurred between actor and character, and we can't tell the two apart. (So many examples come to mind: Cate Blanchett in *Blue Jasmine*, James Gandolfini in *The Sopranos*, Viola Davis in *Ma Rainey's Black Bottom*, Denzel Washington in *Training Day*, Meryl Streep in *Sophie's Choice*, Michael K. Williams in *The Wire*, Zendaya in *Euphoria*. I'm sure you'll come up with your favorites.) This is the goal for every performance and is a transcendent experience for the actor. It rarely happens automatically and sometimes not at all. You may feel different degrees of connection with some scripts and characters than others—which is to be expected. But the exercises in this book endeavor to get you to that connected place in any script you attempt. Note: Do you always have to be viscerally connected to create a successful performance? Not at all. See TECHNIQUE.

GROUNDED — Can be interchangeable with *connected*, in that you may hear the phrase "a grounded performance." It can also mean what you use to achieve a connected performance, for example, "Using my I Believe (Part Two) grounded my audition for the social worker." *Grounded* can also mean bringing reality and grit to a script, so that it feels like we're watching a human being live their life, rather than a character in a story. This style of acting is the lodestar of our best working actors today.

CHARACTER — is the most commonly used word to mean who you are in a script.

Role and *part* are also used. In class I tend to use the word *human* to remind my students that they're not playing a cartoon or caricature, rather a flesh-and-blood human being. For the sake of common understanding, I do use the word *character* in this book, but please always think *human*. Unless you're playing a wizard.

SCRIPT—The written text containing characters (including their descriptions), action, setting, and dialogue that tells a story. (You might hear some old-schoolers interchange the word *text* for script, so be prepared!) I also like characterizing the script as the road map to the character's behavior. Though most of this book is about connecting truthfully to moments in the script, it's important that the actor have a macro understanding of the overall story being told and how their character fits into that story.

SIDES—The page or pages of the script that you receive for your audition. Quite often it's the only portion of the script that you have access to until you book (are hired for) the role.

SETTING—The location where the story takes place, either the entire project (*A Streetcar Named Desire* takes place in New Orleans) or a particular scene (doctor's office).

SUBTEXT—The undercurrent of what is not spoken in a scene. A character could say "I feel great!" when they're feeling the opposite. This behavior can occur due to circumstances or when a character does not feel willing or able to speak their truth. You will see an example in Part One's Everyday + Cover Exercise.

MUSCLE MEMORY—is a phrase I use a lot and is an invaluable tool for actors. Muscle memory is a term that athletes use when they practice certain moves, like a golfer's swing, where, by repetition, the body automatically remembers how to recreate a movement. Actors are emotional athletes, so our muscle memory involves the recreation of behavior or an emotion that we've discovered in these chapters, in rehearsal, or life in general. I believe that emotions from past experiences reside in our body, and with practice, an actor can learn how to access those emotions with their muscle memory skill.

MODE—There is a Mode of Being chapter in the book, but I do mention mode in other contexts. You become a better actor by observing the modes of your behavior. You are in a studious mode while reading this book. You are in a flirtatious mode on a date, and desperation mode running late to catch a flight. Start paying attention to all of these modes to ground yourself and connect to a script. See how these terms start to recycle?

TECHNIQUE—The sum of the actor's skills (e.g., voice, diction, movement, body language, script analysis, muscle memory, emotional recall, etc.). An actor's technique, learned through practice and experience, can carry an actor in a performance, even if they are not experiencing emotional or visceral connection. Working on the exercises in this book will help you develop your technique.

CHARACTER OBJECTIVE — What the human being you are embodying desperately wants in a script. Quite often, it's simply to be loved. Other common objectives are gaining power, survival, or saving one's family or loved ones. Or in Harold and Kumar's case, getting a White Castle burger.

STAKES—The urgency and importance of a given situation. High Stakes = Saving the Earth from alien invasion. Not-So-High Stakes = Saving money on your car insurance.

BEAT — A moment in a scene, usually an action, emotion, new discovery, or anything else that propels the story forward. I believe beats emerge organically with these exercises, but I do cover them in the Actions chapter (Part Three). In auditions or on a set, your colleagues may refer to beats, and it's important that you're aware of the term.

WHAT IF or MAGIC IF—A term credited to Konstantin Stanivslavski (commonly known as the originator of Method Acting) whereby the actor imagines a hypothetical situation and how they would behave in that situation.

FOURTH WALL — A common term used in most acting methods. The fourth wall is the imaginary wall that separates the actor from either the audience or the camera. The term "breaking the fourth wall" means the actor addresses the camera or audience directly.

ACTORY — Even though I thought I made this word up, it actually does exist, meaning "typical of an actor." In my world, the definition is "typical of a *bad* actor," someone who is going through the motions of acting without a real, personal connection. The result is a mechanical or overblown performance. For the love of God, don't be actory—be the most authentic version of you.

F-BOMBS — Not a technical acting term but they do occasionally pop up in these pages. This is not gratuitous and without consideration. My intention is for you to experience what actually transpires in class as if you were there, and sometimes that's a very raw, unsanitized place from which great acting emerges. The reality is, more of our TV and film scripts for all ages reflect this same rawness. This is acting, not a tea party. However, if you were expecting a tea party, I do have one of my mother's favorite finger sandwich recipes in the Appendix. I hope you enjoy it.

PART ONE

THE ESSENTIAL ACTOR

One of the things I like about acting is that, in a funny way, I come back to myself.

—Bill Murray

THE PERSONAL SCENE

A role has to feel personal, because you do your best when you feel the role in your bones.
—Sophia Loren

Almost any acting performance on TV, film, or stage starts with a script. There are more elaborate definitions of what a script is (see Key Terms), but for our purposes now, let's just call it the pieces of paper with your character's action and dialogue.

Since it's difficult to obtain permission to reprint large portions of material from TV and film, here's an example of a script excerpt written especially for this book by my screenwriter husband, Tom Flynn. (Tom was nominated for a 2020 WGA Award by the Writers' Guild of America for Best Original Longform for the movie *Togo*. He's also very handy around the house.) Imagine the following dialogue as if it's written on a piece of paper you're holding in your hand:

```
INT. CHRIS AND TERRY'S APARTMENT - DAY

CHRIS plays a game on the phone
while TERRY paces the room, about to
explode. Then, the eruption …

                TERRY
          You're no friend.

                CHRIS
    I'm a wonderful friend. I've put up
        with you since high school.

                TERRY
       Then go with me. PLEASE!

                CHRIS
    No. You still owe me for the double
             date from hell.
```

TERRY
Do you know what these tickets cost?

CHRIS
Maybe not what they cost but I know what they're worth.

(off Terry's expression)

TERRY
They're for the American Idol concert! Who doesn't want to go to that?

CHRIS
Me! And every other human being in a 500-mile radius who has an ounce of taste.

TERRY
But my boss is going to be there. I'll look like a loser if I show up alone!

CHRIS
Don't worry. Most of the contestants are runners-up. You'll fit right in.

The dialogue plus the setting (Chris and Terry's apartment; INT. is short for interior, EXT. would be exterior) indicate that these are two friends with history, clashing because they want different things in that moment. Can you relate? Of course you can. You've had a friend, lover, spouse, sibling, child, or coworker who you've butted heads with. So, you'd think that anybody could pick up this script and know how to bring it to life. But such is usually not the case.

Why? After much deliberation and meticulous research, I've decided that the script has evil powers.

The act of picking up those flat pieces of paper and speaking the words written on them can turn an otherwise charming human being into a robotic humanoid. In the early days of my classes, my new actors would handle dialogue like a succession of lines to be regurgitated on cue when the other actor stopped talking, moving stiffly about the stage as if riding bareback on a rusted chainsaw, and as soon as the last word left their lips, they would shoot me a look, begging to be put out of their misery.

Even though I tried to explain to my students that the script is merely a road map to human behavior, the point wasn't getting across. But after the Rick Epiphany (in the Prologue, in case you skipped it), I realized the best way for an actor to understand a script was to write their own from their personal experience, thus the Personal Scene exercise was born. This is the first scene every student does in my studio, regardless of previous training, and it becomes a baseline of reference for future scripted scenes.

Like a physical workout that addresses multiple muscle groups, the Personal Scene achieves miraculous results with just about everyone. It taps into your deepest emotional connection, usually with one of your personal cast of characters in your life, which going forward we'll refer to as one of your Hot Persons. It also is likely one of your Hot Situations. (Both will be explained in the next chapter.) This emotional connection will establish a muscle memory that you can call upon at any time in scenes with a similar theme.

It will bring you back to the place where this event happened, Place being an important tool to bring to every scene that you will act in from this day forward.

It helps you embrace the improvisational nature of good acting—which at its best has a spontaneous, unpredictable quality and leaves us on the edge of our seats, wondering what's going to happen next.

It demystifies the script and gets you to recognize it as a living, breathing *road map* to a human experience, rather than just lines in a row to be memorized. So, rather than letting the script have power over you and letting the tail wag the dog, you now understand that you are the one with the power.

Finally, it gives you a feeling of success and catharsis. There's no way you can fail doing this scene— it's your life! And catharsis, because when you are finished, you will feel freer due to this wonderful release you've just experienced. When we watch you, we also experience catharsis. You have just helped us get in touch with our humanity.

That's the beginning of what great acting is all about.

The Personal Scene exercise

Here are the steps of how we approach the Personal Scene in class.

Think of a time in your life when you were deeply, emotionally connected to a person or event or both. It could be a loss, a trauma, a confrontation, an embarrassing event—it could even be a joyful experience. It could also be a conversation/confrontation that did *not* occur but you wish had. How many times have you walked away from a situation muttering to yourself all the things you wish you had said? For example, one of my students chose a fantasy confrontation with his college football coach after he felt he was wrongfully cut from the team.

One or two events may pop up immediately—if they do, choose the one that's the hottest for you, that gets your insides percolating. It's rare when an actor can't think of anything. If you're stuck—take a walk, go to the gym, soak in the tub, eat some chocolate—anything to get your subconscious working for you. Something will come up.

Here are examples of what came up for my students:

- Betsy confronting the hospital staff for their shoddy treatment of her husband
- Alicia saying goodbye to her father on his deathbed (some students have also done fantasy versions of the deathbed scene in case they did not get the chance to say goodbye to a loved one)
- Debra's fantasy confrontation with the client who took her to court
- Sheila's birth of her child
- Roman coming out to their parents
- Gary telling his son he needed to grow up and take responsibility
- Brianna apologizing to her ex for her bad behavior
- Greta's fantasy confrontation with her cheating ex-husband

Simply tell the story of this event, ideally in an acting class, but if you're not in class, then tell a fellow acting student, your acting coach, a trusted confidant, or as a last resort, just sit alone and *say* what happened out loud. I suggest you record it. It's important that you do not try to act this out now or attempt to do dialogue—just describe what happened in chronological order, as if you were simply reporting the facts.

The act of talking about the event out loud is very important because it will start your visceral connection. You will probably recall bits and pieces of what was said, if not entire conversations verbatim, and you will be emotionally transported to the place where the event happened. Like all other strong memories, this will take on a three-dimensional quality so tangible you will feel as if you can reach out and touch it.

Here's an example of the first part of this exercise. My student Debra was a former real estate agent and naturally introverted. She told the story in class of how she had shown a house to a client who apparently had no interest and subsequently bought another house. At the time she had shrugged it off, thinking, *Whatever, happens all the time.* But when Debra and her husband ended up purchasing said house, the client used a loophole in the law to sue her, and she lost in court. Debra had deep, unresolved feelings toward the former client she had never been able to express and was still raw from the experience seven years later.

Now you will write the scene. In my class, the student and I decide what the scene is. The actual scene should be pretty clear, but if it's not, ask yourself, *while I'm telling the story, at what point do I feel the most connected—as in angry, sad, or otherwise emotionally invested?* For example, if the story took place at a parent's deathbed and the actor recalls what was said at the deathbed and events at the funeral afterward, which of those was more potent? The scenario itself is not important and doesn't have to be groundbreaking or original—what's important is your personal connection.

The scene will take place in the location of the event and include the dialogue that actually did take place, or the fantasy version if it's an unresolved issue that you'd love to have a second chance at tackling. When you write the scene, you will write it just like any script—what you say, and what the other person says, stage directions, etc. If you want to work in screenplay format, keep it simple. There are many choices of user-friendly screenwriting software out there that offer free versions. Celtx, StudioBinder, and Highland 2 are some that are currently available.

These scenes should never be longer than three pages. That's usually plenty of time to get to the heart of your personal connection, and this is not meant to be a miniseries. If it's just one or two pages, that's fine.

BIG NOTE: Do *not* write the intellectual, sanitized version. Debra (former real estate agent) wrote her fantasy confrontation about the client who took her to court. While she told the story in class, she was extremely emotional, but when she went home to write it, she backed away from her anger. The scene she brought in was written like a slightly unfavorable Yelp review: "You know, I was disappointed that you chose to sue me. It really wasn't very nice." But what she really wanted to say was, "You *bastard*! You lying, cheating *bastard*! You ruined my life, you almost gave me a heart attack, and I hope you burn in *hell*! *Fuck you*!"

My favorite way to avoid the stiff writing trap is to walk it and talk it. Walk around your room and recreate the conversation as it happened, then transcribe it. Rather than writing it as you think it should be, with a pretty little bow on top, you'll write it as it happened—down and dirty. Same concept applies if you decide to write a fantasy confrontation—imagine the conversation with that person as if it's happening now, and write it immediately while it's fresh.

Here's an excerpt of a Personal Scene that happened in class as a fantasy confrontation:

```
                ACTOR
      Dad. I need to talk to you.

                 DAD
     What do you mean you need to
             talk to me?

                ACTOR
```

I've got a couple of things
that you need to hear.

DAD

I don't have time for that now.

ACTOR

I know. Exactly. You don't have
time. You have always
treated me like I don't matter.

DAD

You better watch your tone when you
talk to me.

ACTOR

You watch YOUR tone when
you talk to ME! If you want to fight now
I'll fight you. Say the word and I will
kick your ass, just like you always
kicked my ass.
And then I will ... I will ... walk out
this door and never come back.

(This scene continued, and the actor finished what he wanted to say to his father. There were no blows exchanged. Any physical contact should always be conducted with full knowledge and permission from the scene partner and should always include rehearsal and fight choreography.)

Now you will perform the scene, ideally in an acting class, but you can also get a group of other interested acting students or friends. As a last resort, you can do this alone if it's a monologue.

Do *not* memorize it—I want you to have the feeling of having the script in your hand the first time around. One or more actors will be reading the other part or parts as needed.

Depending on your previous acting experience, the first time you perform this scene, you will notice you may be looking at your script to grab a line here and there. I've noticed many beginning students with their eyes glued to the script as if it's a life raft to save them from drowning—even though it's a scene that they've written!

When the scene is over, take a gut check. Did you feel the same or similar connection as when you were retelling the event? Make a mental note of how you felt.

Now you will put the script down and perform the scene again. Don't panic—you will remember it because this is your life! You may not say the words as perfectly as you wrote them, but I can almost guarantee whatever comes out of your mouth will be more authentic than the first version. The lines may actually take on a more unpredictable, improvised quality, as if it's happening for the first time. *You are now recreating the scene not tied to your script but connected to the event, to your memories, and to your emotional truth.* That is the goal of great acting.

> When you work with a professional script, you must perform the lines as written but you can still use this technique. During your rehearsal process, put the script down and improvise the gist of the scene, then go back to the actual text. This will help you bring the words to life and make you shine in an audition. The lines are important, but more important is your essence, your connection, *you!*

In a case like Debra's where the written script doesn't match the truth, I'll have the actor throw the script away and direct them to improvise from their gut on the spot. In Debra's case, she found her voice the second time around and spoke (screamed) all the unsaid things she wanted to say to the client. It was not only an amazing cathartic experience for all of us in the room, but I saw seven years of grief lifted off her shoulders.

Most students feel somewhat connected during the first performance of this scene. During the second version, I can safely say that almost everyone experiences an amazing transformation. They lose their self-consciousness because they have a true personal connection to the script. They forget to worry about the "lines," not only because they are the author, but also because they now realize that the scene is about the relationship with the other human being and what they want from them. *The lines are just the vehicle they use to get what they need from the other person.*

I want to emphasize the intention of this exercise. This is not about being self-indulgent or to imply that good acting is always a screaming match or a pity party. But it is our job to tell the story of our characters truthfully, and some may experience onc or many strong emotional moments. I have found this exercise to be the most effective way to not only reach those moments organically but to achieve total freedom on stage.

Imagine if you felt that kind of freedom and connection with someone else's words, aka *the script?* Now that you've told your story in your own words, you have the power to tell the story of other characters in the same real way. This exercise is just the beginning of how you will connect with scripts, with roles large and small, whether you have one hour or one month to prepare. You can repeat the Personal Scene as many times as you desire, creating scenes about different scenarios in your life. This exercise gives you the key to be your most authentic, truthful self in almost any emotionally challenging scene you will tackle in your working actor career.

A final note about the Personal Scene

While the majority of my students have found this exercise to be game-changing in terms of connection, catharsis, and their overall understanding of approaching scripts, a small percentage find revisiting personal events intrusive and opt to sit it out. That's always okay. Let me be very clear—you are always in charge of your craft and what you choose to bring to it or keep private— for this book, for classes, and for any job you choose to accept or decline. Always remember that for the rest of your career!

HOT BUTTONS

The better I am at observing moments in life, the better I'll be at showing them in my acting.
—Oscar Isaac

The concept of substitution is very common in most acting methods—it simply means to imagine a human being from your life as the character you're interacting with in a scene. (If you're wondering, "Why can't I just use the actor I'm already in the scene with?" the answer is, you can. For now, I'm preparing you to be brilliant, even if your scene partner is a stone pillar. Which some of them are.)

The point of substitution in acting is how it changes your behavior and informs your choices in a scene and in this, art imitates life. Because *you* modify your behavior, or in some cases become a totally different human being, depending on whom you are interacting with and what the situation is. You would behave differently in a business transaction as opposed to a first date (or at least I hope you would). And that behavior further changes according to the circumstances of the situation—is the person in the business transaction a partner who betrayed you? Or the first date the potential love of your life? In real life, these factors—the situation and the other human being—affect your behavior and your emotional responses. These Hot Buttons are a powerful way of putting your own stamp on things. They bring freshness to the scene and make it seem immediate, like we're eavesdropping on a real event.

Going forward, for every scene in every script you ever do for the rest of your life, you must identify the types of characters and relationships in your scripted material and find your corresponding real-life person who best fits the situation. In class, I call this substitution the Hot Person. To be clear, the word "hot" isn't to be confused with sexy hot, but rather to convey the raw and immediate chemical reaction that hits your gut when you have an image of interacting with this person. You will have not only that reaction, but you will also notice a change in your posture, your tone of voice, and your body language, among other natural physical adjustments. These all become part of your *muscle memory* that will be one of your most important tools.

So, who are the Hot Persons in your life? Here's where your life experience comes in handy. They are the people who conjure up the strongest emotional reactions in you, from your earliest years to the present. These emotions, memories, and reactions can range from warmly intimate and nurturing to extreme rage.

It's more than likely that the other human beings in your Personal Scene are major players in this cast that you will keep in your mental files from now on. They can include parents, grandparents, a boyfriend, girlfriend, partner, husband or wife, exes, children, bosses, coworkers, authority figures, the rude teller at the bank this morning, the guy who cut you off in traffic, loud neighbors, your high school crush, your first pet. I've also had students use famous people like Nancy Pelosi and Leonardo DiCaprio.

This list will ebb and flow. What was hot today may not work tomorrow. Some will always be hot for you. Your job as an actor is to constantly take your Hot Person temperature and keep the hottest in your stable, ready to go.

When we begin to do scene work in my studio, or when I'm coaching an actor for an audition, one of the first things I ask is: who is the Hot Person? Based on the circumstances in the scene—who in your personal life stirs up similar emotions, sensations, and reactions in you that your character is experiencing? Who will give you the strongest connection possible appropriate for the objective of this scene? Is the situation warm and intimate, confrontational, a business transaction?

Now we start to do the digging. In the beginning, this takes practice and can involve some trial and error. One common mistake is to make a literal apples-to-apples choice—for example, in a scene between spouses to feel obligated to use your own spouse as your Hot Person. An actress may be in an emotional breakup scene with her husband, accusing him of distant and abusive behavior, and demanding a divorce. If the scene seems limp, we may discover she's using her current husband but everything about hubby is great! So, then the question becomes—who is the person, past or present, who has made you feel hurt and angry for not giving you what you need? Ahhh, the ex-boyfriend from five years ago? The parent who called you demeaning names in your childhood? And which one of those provokes the stronger reaction? The parent! Now we'll use that in the scene and watch a completely different, more connected version than ever before.

Quite often, a scene's success is simply a result of choosing the most potent Hot Person. The hottest choice can make your performance authentic and unique by the muscle memory and spontaneous behavior that happens organically in your interplay with this person. If it's a flirtatious or intimate relationship, you may find yourself fiddling with your hair, laughing softly, or discovering any other singular physical behavior that you engage in with this person. If it's a contentious relationship, you will feel your face, body, and tone of voice change. If it's a business relationship, depending on your status and your role in the transaction, you may find yourself in the spectrum of pleasantly accommodating to quietly authoritative.

To see how it works, try this mini exercise right now by yourself. You will be working with a very short script. Ready?

YOU
Hello.

Now sit in a chair, close your eyes, and think of someone who you're wildly attracted to. When you open your eyes, imagine they're sitting in a chair opposite you. "See" their face, make eye contact, even reach out and touch their face if you dare. However they're affecting you, let yourself be affected. Now say your line and imagine their reaction.

Try it again, but this time, close your eyes and imagine someone who you are currently angry with. Go through the same steps, open your eyes, take them in, and say the same line.

Can you see how powerfully this tool works and how even a simple one-word bit of dialogue like "Hello" has so much nuance depending on who the other human is?

The Hot Person also brings relationship history to a scene when it's needed. It can be a friend or family member who you've known your entire life, an ex, a reconnection with an acquaintance from your past. I know some actors find it necessary to write pages and pages of character history when working on a scene, which I'm not against. But many times, the appropriate Hot Person brings all of that same history to your work and has true significance to you, rather than a fictionalized version of your character's life.

When you interact with your Hot Persons, notice not only the emotions they stir up in you but also where you're feeling them in your body. Usually, actors feel certain emotions in different places: their gut, chest, solar plexus, arms. Wherever you're feeling it—make a note and remember it. This will serve as an important tool in your muscle memory.

If you find even one that works over and over again, use it. There are no awards for variety here and no expiration date on what works. Human relationships are complicated, and if one person makes you laugh, cry, angry, jealous, and turns you on ... good for you! There's nothing better than a one-stop shop Hot Person in your life.

As you continue to work on these exercises, you will achieve more emotional flexibility, and without even thinking about it, these will all be at your fingertips at the drop of a hat. It's a powerful tool to possess, whether you're working on a new scene in class or in a callback with a casting director who wants you to conjure up a new emotional color on a dime. If you're the actor who can deliver—that may be the winning factor that books you the job.

HOT BUTTON EXERCISE #1 — YOUR HOT PERSONS

Think of the following:

- *With whom are you the most emotionally relaxed and intimate?*
- *Who do you need to protect and nurture?*
- *Who hurt you terribly and never made amends?*
- *Who do you have a total lack of respect for?*
- *With whom do you have a hot sexual chemistry?*
- *Who makes you the happiest?*
- *Who has royally pissed you off?*
- *Who needs your compassion now?*
- *Who intimidates you?*
- *Who can you tell your deepest secrets to?*
- *Who did you hurt and need to make amends to?*
- *Who or what makes you laugh the silliest?*
- *For whom do you need to be the most professional and do the best job?*
- *Who inspires you?*
- *Who are you jealous of?*
- *Whom do you idolize?*

- *Which friend really lets you be yourself?*
- *Who makes you fearful and/or extremely uncomfortable?*
- *Who is beneath you in status?*
- *Who is higher than you in status?*
- *Who requires the most patience?*
- *Whom do you need to confront about unfinished business?*
- *Whom do you need to confront about treating you badly?*
- *Who has stood in the way of your dreams or goals?*

You don't need to have a different person for each of these—some of your answers may overlap. That's perfectly fine. Some actors may only find two or three strong responses. The point is, what works for you?

I asked you to think, but what I really want you to do is *feel*. Take a walk or do some physical activity while you're asking yourself these questions. Do a constant gut check to feel who pops up and gets the strongest response from you. This will be the beginning of your Hot Person cast that you can start using in your work. Some may be just as strong today as they will be ten years from now. My mother and I had a complicated relationship, and she will always be my Hot Person for her hurtful behavior that remained unresolved at the time of her death. And to this day, I've used her for many a successful audition.

Your Hot Person cast will shift and change, much as your life most certainly will. For example, you may be caring for a young child whom you feel strongly about protecting and nurturing now. In the future, when they're in adulthood, you will of course still love them, but at that time you may have an aging parent in assisted living who needs nurturing and protection, or an ailing pet who needs extra care. (Yes, I've actually substituted my four-legged family members in place of humans for a strong emotional connection. If your fur relationships are as strong as your human ones, I'm sure you can relate.)

Remember, this is your Hot Person, not your Lukewarm Person. You need to always make the hottest choice—someone you have the strongest reaction to. You may have a spouse who easily fits the circumstance of being at ease, relaxed, and content, but they may not be the best choice for hot sexual chemistry. Married people might feel guilty admitting this in class, but your truth is your truth! One of my married students needed a hot sexual chemistry choice for an awkward should-we-or-should-we-not-kiss-on-the-doorstep dating scene and immediately dismissed using her husband, as she knew any inherent danger or sexual tension no longer existed after twenty years of marriage. And she didn't have any real-life crushes outside of her marriage that she could use. I asked her—who of anyone in the world would turn her on if they stood on the doorstep with her? She giggled and said, "Brad Pitt." I told her to try it—and it worked! We watched her transform from stiff and indifferent to blushing and stuttering when we discovered that Brad and only Brad could get that reaction from her. This is also a great reminder that if nobody in your life is working, use your imagination (especially if your imagination likes shirtless, award-winning actors).

I suggest you keep a log of your Hot Persons, both real and imaginary, and save it on your computer or whatever note-saving device you have. If someone new pops up, add them. Keep this list current and refer to it often. It comes in handy for those eleventh-hour auditions when you're under the gun and need to jog your gut to make the hottest choice possible.

So, be grateful for the cheating ex who dumped you, the coworker who stabbed you in the back, or the jerk who cut you off on the freeway. That's a perk of the job. Rather than binge eating, drinking, or other self-destructive behavior other human beings do to cope with painful feelings—you can consider yourself lucky because they will become gold for your art. Thank them all when you accept your Academy Award.®

Hot Button exercise #2 — observing your behavior with your Hot Persons

Start taking note of your everyday interactions. For example, with your significant other, pay attention to your exchanges ranging from normal chitchat to playful, sillier subjects to sincere declarations of love. Note your body language, tone of voice, and every other detail that pops up.

Note how you are at work—how you interact with your boss, with your coworkers and/or customers. How do your mood, mannerisms, and tone of voice differ from interactions with other people and situations in your life?

Note how you are with friends—either one on one or in a party situation. Our own dynamics can change according to our friends' personalities; note how you are with the talkative alpha friend as opposed to a quieter friend. Even these subtle differences in relationships can be an effective Hot Person tool in a scene.

File all of these observations in your personal notebook, and be specific. They will come in handy when you begin your scene work.

Hot Button exercise #3 — Hot Person mini-scene

This exercise must be done with another actor in order to be effective. You are practicing endowing another human as your Hot Person to see how that affects your visceral connection and how it changes your behavior.

Set up two chairs, with your fellow actor filling in as your Hot Person sitting in one of the chairs, ideally facing a door where you will be entering. You have the first line and the last line, with the Hot Person responding in the middle.

Choose these three Hot Persons from your answers above:

- *Hot Person #1. Who makes you fearful or uncomfortable?*
- *Hot Person #2. Whom do you need to nurture?*
- *Hot Person #3. With whom do you have hot sexual chemistry?*

Now I will give you lines that you will use to interact with your Hot Person. (There are more of these mini-scenes in the Appendix.)

You: Do you have a moment?
Hot Person: Not now, I'm busy.
You: I think you really need to listen.

You will choose Hot Person #1 and use those lines. I have my actors do this exercise entering and exiting the stage to experience how differently they move and how their body language changes with each person. Don't plan whether you'll sit or stand—that will unfold organically depending on your emotional connection in the moment. After your last line, don't drop the connection but hold it with the other actor. When we repeat this exercise with my more experienced actors, I encourage them to improvise and continue the conversation, and that can result in an exciting scene.

Now you will repeat the scene using the same lines, but with Hot Person #2. And once more with Hot Person #3.

Notice the lines are neutral and the situation is nondescript. That's the point—this exercise is not about the script, scene objective, or performance. It's just about you discovering how radically *you* change according to your Hot Person. You will notice the difference in your visceral connection, your voice, and your body language with each one. Notice also how the delivery of the lines changes, as if we're watching three different scenes.

(A note for the actor filling in for Hot Person: let your partner drive the scene. You are not obligated to do anything but respond naturally to what your partner gives you.)

A great side benefit to this exercise is, just like the Personal Scene, the actor experiences freedom with a given script, rather than feeling controlled and constricted by the dialogue. A mistake many beginning actors make is a snap judgment about the reading of a particular line. That's the Tail Wagging the Dog version of acting. You can see how many different ways you can say, "I think you really need to listen" according to the Hot Person that you're interacting with. Rather than the on-the-nose version of nagging or complaining, it can be tender, or flirtatious, or even sexy. When dealing with the person who needs to make amends with you, it can be an empathetic plea. It's a great lesson that will distinguish your acting performance from the actors who would read the same lines in the most cliched and unimaginative way possible.

I realize that some schools of acting dictate that your performance is dependent on what you get from the other actor. While that would be wonderful in a perfect world where the other actor is Denzel Washington and you're getting something meaty to react off of, many times that's not the case. That's especially true in auditions with a reader or casting director who may not be giving you something to work with. Or if you're cast with another actor with whom you have zero chemistry. This exercise puts the power back in your corner, so it doesn't matter what you're getting—you are still behaving according to your Hot Person choice.

You may be able to use your imagination to actually *see* the Hot Person in a scene. But don't expect that or think you've failed because you do not. The Hot Person gives you the gut connection to start the scene and puts you in the appropriate emotional place where you need to be. Ideally it will give you enough momentum to carry you through and achieve your objective. Using this tool is one of the most game-changing components for your career as a working actor.

Hot Button exercise #4 — your Hot Situation list

There are events you've experienced in your life that evoke an emotional memory but don't necessarily involve another specific person, or if they did, the situation itself is more significant than the people involved. For example, when I fainted on the street in Los Angeles and woke up surrounded by EMTs and passersby (don't worry—I was just dehydrated, and I lived to write this book), the people weren't significant in my memory, but the event itself was. This is what I call a **Hot Situation**.

Some examples of **Hot Situations** are:

- 9/11
- Losing your car keys
- Opening your college acceptance letter
- Running into a snake in your backyard
- Watching fireworks or any other visual spectacle
- Being stuck in an elevator
- Hiking in the mountains
- Winning a medal or prize for an achievement
- Getting lost in a foreign city
- Seeing your favorite band in concert

Some Personal Scenes are more about an event than a relationship and are also examples of Hot Situations. These events can be loaded with a range of emotions: fear, frustration, anger, wonder, joy, embarrassment. The intensity of emotion can range from extreme to more nuanced. (Don't discount the situations where the emotions are more subtle and nuanced. They can be just as valuable and will also be great assets for you when you start working on film.)

Keep a running list of any of these Hot Situations that you can recall now and as they happen to you. You will likely remember how you felt by just writing the name of the event, for example, *Stepped in dog poop in Manhattan*, but in case you need more of a memory jog you can write key words like "frustrated" "disgusted" etc.

If you would like to experiment how a Hot Situation can affect your inner life and your behavior, pick a spot on the wall and imagine you're seeing the most breathtaking fireworks display, or whatever your ideal visual spectacle is. See the colors, the details, even the smells if appropriate. Let all of this affect you, and savor the feeling. And if you want to go deeper, switch to another Hot Situation, maybe desperately looking for your keys, passport, or something you would need if you're late and leaving on vacation. Feel it? We're not even working on a script yet, but you can see how you can drop into your character's life just by using this extremely effective tool.

BIG NOTE: If you audition for commercials, quite often there will be no dialogue, just reactions to something you're only seeing in your imagination (like fireworks). USE THIS HOT SITUATION TOOL, and you will likely be among the top casting candidates!

Hot Button exercise #5 — Hot Person Confrontation

If you're human, you've likely had the experience of repressing your feelings in a difficult interaction with another person. But rather than speaking your truth, you walked away fuming with your unspoken comeback boiling in your gut. Anybody else, or just me?

One of the reasons why we love dramatic shows is we live vicariously through our favorite characters' beautifully written, cathartic confrontations. There are a multitude of moments in plays, TV, and film where a character confronts one or many other characters. These can range from a quiet exchange to the emotional climax of the piece. A confrontation can occur within an intimate relationship, a courtroom, a classroom, a battlefield, a boardroom, in any working environment, and a multitude of other scenarios.

To be clear—this isn't a physical confrontation. It's a speech or dialogue to achieve a goal, whether it be to change another character's behavior, to demand an apology, to extract a confession, to have a catharsis, to exert or take back one's own power in a relationship among many possible circumstances.

If you're connected, this exercise will most likely stir up feelings of anger. In modern society, anger is usually considered a negative emotion that most people shy away from. If you look up quotes about anger, it's called everything from paralyzing to poisonous. And yes, unchecked and uncontrolled anger can lead to dangerous consequences and should not be taken lightly.

However, I believe if anger is channeled for one's art, it can be one of the most powerful tools at your disposal. Your anger can be a positive force, especially if used as fuel to propel you through these moments of confrontation and many other moments in your scene work—both dramatic and comedic.

Think of our great working actors right now. Remember Julia Roberts in *Erin Brockovich*? Jennifer Lawrence in *Silver Linings Playbook*? Jack Nicholson in *A Few Good Men*? Charlize Theron in *Monster* and *Atomic Blonde*? Al Pacino in *Scent of a Woman, Angels in America, The Godfather*, and the rest of his filmography? Great actors don't shy away from using anger; rather they use it frequently, knowing it makes their performances dynamic and unique.

In class, I've seen my actors struggle with expressing their authentic anger. I usually find out they've previously been shamed, or concerned they'll be perceived as unattractive or afraid of what would happen if they lose control. As an acting teacher, I have a responsibility that my students do no harm to themselves or others, but within those boundaries, I encourage my students to lose control—to go "there." They not only overcome their fear but find a new sense of self-empowerment. And it makes for exciting moments in a scene.

Think of a Hot Person in your life whom you need to confront and speak your truth. This situation could be anything, including an unresolved abusive relationship with a parent, sibling, or other family member, an ex, a teacher, a boss. It can even be an incident with a stranger that was left unresolved.

Once you've found the Hot Person, start talking to them. Unlike the Personal Scene, this should not be written but improvised. It's best if you have an actor standing in as your Hot Person that you're confronting. That actor doesn't need to contribute much to the conversation, but if they do, it's helpful if they understand an outline of the situation so they don't deny your reality. The bulk of the dialogue does not rest with them however—it mostly comes from you.

This can be done alone if necessary. You can imagine this Hot Person sitting in a chair or standing across a room. What's important is you feeling free to speak your truth.

Note the temperature of your confrontation. Was it at high volume, did it bring color to your face and make your heart palpitate? Or was it quiet and controlled? There is no right answer—just something for you to make note of. If it was one or the other, now find a Hot Person who would elicit a different type of emotional response. If you had a big, dramatic *FUCK YOU* showdown with your ex, try a confrontation of another flavor—perhaps a restrained encounter with a boss or coworker. Stockpile all of these different tones in your palette and start to recognize how they can be utilized in different scenarios. All of these will add variety in the choices you will be able to access for future work.

Anytime you need to rekindle this connection before a scene or an audition, you can do this exercise alone—in your head or out loud in your room, in your car, in the shower. But please don't do it in the audition room. No one is interested in your process; they just want to see the result.

NOTES FROM CLASS ABOUT THIS EXERCISE:

There have been so many great examples of riveting Hot Person Confrontations in class that I have to share. One of my favorites is my student Marvin confronting his college football coach who had cut him from the team and derailed his chances to make the pro leagues. I wish we had recorded this confrontation! His scene was a perfect example of the many colors that anger can take in a confrontation. There was authentic hurt, rage and even sarcastic humor that Marvin expressed brilliantly. The takeaway is if you're using *you*—anger is not necessarily a one-note emotion but can be multifaceted.

Another example is my student Marsha, who had always struggled with any scene that required her to express anger. She's a gentle soul who believes in harmony and forgiveness and doesn't like to acknowledge any emotion she perceives as negative. At climactic angry moments in a scene, her voice would take on a fake, strained quality, which was the best she could do to approximate the real thing. However, with this exercise, she confronted her brother's significant other for causing his estrangement from the family, an issue that had been deeply troubling her for years but she had been afraid to address. For the first time, she was able to experience a real connection to her truthful self; her voice was powerful, and her scene work has skyrocketed ever since.

The remarkable aspect of this exercise is how it's subject to one's own interpretation. My version of a confrontation might be fiery and charged with emotion. Another actor might have an entirely different mode of expression. One of my students, in confronting his mother, never raised his voice. He had a smile on his face the entire time, but the words he was saying were, "You make me sick. I hate you." Imagine if an actor brought that interpretation to a written script—how refreshing that would be for the casting people. A truthful yet bold choice like that would definitely stand out in an audition.

Hot Button exercise #6 — Hot Person Confrontation in scene work

In class, if there is a confrontational moment in a scene, as there often is, and if my actor is struggling, as many of my beginners do, we'll stop the scene immediately and do the basic improvised Hot Person Confrontation Exercise. Then they'll go back to the script and redo the confrontational moment, using the *muscle memory* they've just created with the given dialogue in the script. It works miracles almost every time—like seeing a new actor in a new scene.

You can experience how this can transform your performance by following the same steps. I've obtained permission to reprint this key excerpt from one of the great American plays, *The Glass Menagerie* by Tennessee Williams. It's a classic confrontation between Tom and Amanda. Amanda is Tom's mother and is desperately fighting for her family's survival in 1930s New Orleans. Tom, who yearns to escape his circumstances, is the sole breadwinner of the household, as his father abandoned them long ago. Tom's sister, Laura (a recluse whose childhood illness left her with a limp), is not in the scene but is another burden to him and contributes to his frustration and desire for freedom. Read the following scene with a scene partner:

THE GLASS MENAGERIE

PART I
SCENE THREE

TOM
What in Christ's name am I—

AMANDA [shrilly]
Don't you use that—

TOM
—supposed to do!

AMANDA
—expression! Not in my—

TOM
Ohhh!

AMANDA
—presence! Have you gone out of your senses?

TOM
I have, that's true, *driven* out!

AMANDA
What is the matter with you, you—big—big—IDIOT!

TOM
Look!—I've got *no thing*, no single thing—

AMANDA
Lower your voice!

TOM
—in my life here that I can call my OWN! Everything is—

AMANDA
Stop that shouting!

TOM
Yesterday you confiscated my books! You had the nerve to—

AMANDA
I took that horrible novel back to the library—yes! That hideous book by the insane Mr. Lawrence. [Tom laughs wildly] I cannot control the output of diseased minds or people who cater to them—[Tom laughs still more wildly] BUT I WON'T ALLOW SUCH FILTH BROUGHT INTO MY HOUSE! No, no, no, no, no!

TOM
House, house! Who pays rent on it, who makes a slave of himself to—

AMANDA
[Fairly screeching]
Don't you DARE to—

TOM
No, no, *I* mustn't say things! *I've* got to just—

AMANDA
Let me tell you—

TOM
I don't want to hear any more!

This scene is very difficult to do without gas in your tank. This is where the Hot Person Confrontation exercise can be very helpful.

I don't want to do this play a disservice by implying it's not complex material. The common agreement is Tom's character is gay, and this argument is loosely shrouding Amanda's disgust, disapproval, but also fear of losing him and Tom's yearning to be free of her and live an authentic life. That could be important information, especially in choosing a Hot Person. But even without that information, we can use the dialogue to demonstrate how this exercise can give you the visceral connection you need—in this case to win a highly charged argument—and can be the start of future work on this and other similar scripts.

First of all, if you're playing Tom, how would you choose your Hot Person for Amanda? If you say your mother, that could be true, or it could be a trap. How does Amanda treat Tom? She demeans him, doesn't accept him, does not let him be his authentic self, makes him feel stifled. So, you in turn must think of a person who demeans you, who doesn't accept you or allow you to be authentic, who has made you miss opportunities. Somebody who has power over you from whom you yearn to break free.

If you're Amanda, who is your Hot Person? This is where it becomes imperative not to judge the character you're playing. Your worldview may not at all be the same as Amanda's, especially about the acceptance of her gay son. Your job is to not to judge her but to ask yourself, how does she respond, communicate, and react to Tom? The human being who Tom represents could be someone who's disappointed you, someone whose behavior disgusts you, someone who's let you down when you've needed them the most, and at the same time someone who you don't want to let go of. It could be an alcoholic or drug addict, a compulsive liar, an ex who cheated on you.

Both actors need to choose someone who makes them boil. This is not a logical or reasoned discourse but rather a tantrum, a catharsis. You need to use this confrontation as a way to get the other person *to feel the pain that they've inflicted upon you*.

Now improvise the Hot Person Confrontation with this Hot Person and go full throttle. Notice the change in your body, and make note of that muscle memory.

Next pick up the script, using the same muscle memory with the given dialogue, and see what happens. You will notice there are many times when the characters cut each other off. If that happens organically with you—bravo! In a real confrontation where we are connected to our truth and anger, there is no such thing as politely waiting for the other person to stop speaking, and Tennessee Williams has indicated by his punctuation that this is that type of confrontation. As actors, we of course rehearse this, but in the performance, if we're connected and using our muscle memory, the scene will seem fresh and spontaneous every time.

Even though this is difficult material to master, the Hot Person Confrontation tool will give you the fuel to propel you through this scene and other scenes like it for the rest of your career.

EVERYDAY SCENE

Good actors are always looking for props. They're looking for behavior.
It makes it a lot easier. You're not solely dependent of what's coming out of your mouth.
You're also less self-conscious, less aware of the camera.
—Peter Falk

One of the biggest misconceptions I've heard from both new and experienced actors is that brilliant acting has to feel like extreme effort. Some actors think they're failing unless they have gnashing teeth, bulging forehead veins, or rivulets of sweat pouring from their armpits during a scene. "Do less," I'll say. "But it doesn't feel like I'm working at all," they'll complain. "Yes!" I reply, *"that's exactly how you should feel!"*

Even though we call acting "work," we're not at the gym bench pressing 300-pound barbells, we're recreating human behavior. Unless you're running from an asteroid or fighting zombies, quite often that behavior is extremely ordinary or what I've identified as Everyday. Does your Everyday behavior feel like work? No. It's natural, real. It's you living your life authentically.

Turn on your TV set now and flip through the channels. Notice how many scenes portray simple human interaction, even if they're tucked between more dramatic moments. As an actor and acting coach, I can attest that these simple human interactions are abundant in movie and TV scripts and are quite common in audition material. Will you still occasionally read for the anguished parent, the betrayed spouse, or the screaming army captain? Sure. But trust me, this Everyday tone is so ubiquitous—and so important for you to embrace now—that I've included it as one of the Essential tools in Part One. There are more scenes in this mode than you realize, and the sooner you learn to identify them, the more roles you will win.

You may have read a critically favorable review about an acting performance that mentions the word "real" or "effortless." It's when the acting is so authentic, it seems unrehearsed and improvised. (Frances McDormand in *Nomadland* is a great example.) That's the goal for any performance, but especially when the tone of the movie or TV show is of a more naturalistic style.

One of my favorite examples of an actor in an Everyday moment is Amy Ryan's performance in *Dan in Real Life*. Amy plays Steve Carell's sister-in-law, one of a large family all gathered at the parents' home in Rhode Island. In a scene where various family members are circulating in the kitchen, Amy's character is occupied with preparing a meal and interacting with them as they enter and exit. She is engrossed with the task at hand, and you never catch her acting. It's wonderful work.

A scene can also start in Everyday mode before it explodes into a crisis or confrontation, like the flashback scene in *Dolores Claiborne*, which begins as a conversation in the kitchen between Kathy Bates and David Straitharn and ends with her pulling a knife on him.

I strongly believe I booked the role of Joan in the film *High Expectations* because I immediately recognized the tone of my one-on-one scene with my fiancé Coach Harrison Davis (played by Kelsey Grammer) as Everyday. We are in our kitchen, where Joan is listening and empathizing with him while making sandwiches. There is a great deal of emotional content, but the key is we are two people having an intimate conversation, completely relaxed in the other's presence.

In class I noticed that my students were finding this Everyday tone even more difficult than the big, dramatic moments. Any scene requiring normal human interaction coupled with a simple task that should be second nature looked like a Herculean effort. The actors would push, over-perform or make a *thing* out of it—"Look at me, I'm making *coffee*!" On stage or on a set, if this self-consciousness bleeds through—in other words, if we catch you acting—the scene is unsuccessful and it takes us out of the story.

Whereas the Personal Scene was created for actors to connect to an extraordinary moment, I introduced the Everyday Scene exercise in class to remind my students of their natural behavior in an ordinary moment. What is it like when you do something simple that should be second nature and bring it to the stage? What is it like to just "be," as if there was no camera rolling and no audience? Whereas some acting schools do relaxation exercises before scene work, these exercises teach your body to relax *while* you're acting. They lock that behavior into your muscle memory, which you can replicate at an audition or on a set. As an actor, it's vital to be as skillful at handling the small moments as the big ones—and understanding the difference will make writers, directors, and audiences fall in love with you.

Everyday Scene exercise #1

Pay attention to a regular, mundane activity you do every day that involves an interaction or conversation with one other person, for example making and eating breakfast with your significant other, friend, or roommate. Other examples: gathering your items together to start your workday while talking about the day ahead, getting your kid ready to go to school, a casual interaction with a coworker. Note the effortless way you talk to this person, your body language. Note how easily the activity comes to you without even thinking about it. It's important that your activity involves at least one or several items (aka props) like dishes, laundry, paper and pencil, etc. that you must deal with while you're interacting.

Just like the Personal Scene, write it in script form. To be clear, you are playing yourself and not writing this as a character, so if your name is Mary, don't name yourself Belinda in the script. Do not add anything dramatic, such as demanding a divorce from your spouse. The objective is to be as ordinary as possible. For example:

```
YOU
(entering kitchen)
Morning, honey.

THEM
Morning.

YOU
Where's the cat?

THEM
Still sleeping on the bed.

YOU
(opening cupboard)
Want some coffee?

THEM
Sure.
```

YOU
Hey, while you're out today, can you pick up some of that 2% milk at the store?

THEM
What 2% milk?

YOU
(shows carton)
This. Make sure it's the green container.

Now perform this with another human being. You can choose someone who's similar to your real-life partner, although sometimes in class I will suggest a student who is *not* like the other person in the scene. This forces the actor to be able to recreate their natural behavior, regardless of who the scene partner is.

Notice the difference, if any, between your behavior on and off stage. The goal is to feel as real and natural in the performance as you do in your life. If you did, then you experienced an example of how the Everyday scene can ground you and make your acting more believable.

The props are important in this exercise because we are constantly dealing with objects while interacting with other humans, so make sure you use the same objects in the scene that you do in life. One student did his Everyday Scene walking into his workplace empty-handed, and he seemed awkward talking to his coworkers. I stopped the scene and asked if he usually brought a briefcase or satchel to work, and he said yes. When he did the scene again, he carried the briefcase in and started unpacking it as he usually does in the morning. Now he seemed relaxed and in the moment, as if he was really at work.

In my acting roles, I've opened bottles of beer, prepared breakfast, taken notes on a tablet, set up a buffet table, handled a gun, driven a car, put on make-up, thrown darts, displayed pages on an easel, juggled textbooks, all while having a conversation. Yeah? So what? The point is, on a set, under lights, doing dialogue under pressure to get a clean take, these simple activities can feel like walking on a tightrope with high heels, especially for a new actor. The more accustomed you are to working with props, the more confident you will be when you start to work on a set or on stage.

Now that you're paying attention to your natural behavior and the everyday objects you use in certain situations, start noticing all the places where it's appropriate in your scene work and auditions—where all that's required of you is to be real, present, and believable. When you master this effortless style, your auditions will stand out. The true mark of a professional actor is one who we never catch in the act of acting.

Everyday Scene + Cover exercise #2

This is one of my favorite newer exercises, introducing the concept of subtext and working in layers—in other words we are feeling one way yet behaving another or "covering." It uses elements of the Hot Person Confrontation—if the confrontation can't happen at that moment. This exercise helps you find more nuance in your behavior, which in turn adds much more intrigue and nuance to your scenes—one of the keys of on-camera acting.

Think of a Hot Person with whom you currently are at odds—this should be a close relationship. They may have recently said or done something that's hurt you, or you may be considering ending the relationship. If you don't currently have a situation like this, think of something in the recent past or use a "what if?" with someone you care deeply about.

You now will write the scene interacting with this person like an Everyday scene—**without confrontation, discussing the problem, or ending the relationship**—just everyday dialogue like Exercise #1. Bring in an activity with props that you need to accomplish, such as preparing a meal, doing your taxes, putting on make-up, folding laundry, etc., which is what you'll be doing while performing the scene.

The temptation might be to "show" your anger to the audience, like slamming your skillet or barking at your scene partner. Don't. Repress it and keep it internal. The camera is an amazing device—it reads our thoughts so there's no need to telegraph what you're thinking. Record this exercise on your smartphone and watch the playback to see what I mean. If you pushed it or overacted, you'll see it.

Now when you do your scene work—look for the moments where your character may be covering a deep emotion and yet acting as if all is well. When you use the cover, you will add an irresistible level of sophistication to your acting.

WATCH YOUR TONE!

Tone is so important. Is this a thriller, is this a Gothic romance, is this an action film, is this a love story? Then, once I understand that, I just jump into it.
—Tom Hiddleston

Up to this point, the chapters in this section have been about getting you on your feet to audition, using a variety of moments from your life—ranging from personal to everyday. Now that you've experienced some basic connection techniques, we're going to switch gears from your bones to your brain to the very important topic of tone, which I think is essential knowledge for every working actor. Here's why.

Years ago, I did a workshop in Los Angeles for a casting director who was well known for casting comedies. In this workshop, the actors were assigned a script and a scene partner the day of, which we would then perform in front of the entire class. My scene was a semi-funny sketch between two rival TV news anchors, which I knew could be improved with a great comedic performance. I wanted to impress this casting director and couldn't wait to sink my teeth into it.

We were given fifteen minutes to rehearse with our scene partners. My partner was male, average looking, and just tall enough so he could look down his nose at me. This was so long ago I don't remember his name, but let's call him Dick. His first words to me were said in one breath like a hyphenated sentence: "I'm-Dick-and-I-just-graduated-from-A-Very-Prestigious-Acting School-moved-here-last-week-got-an-agent-and-I'm-called-back-to-network-for-a-pilot." Man, that was impressive.

We began reading the script, and after the first few lines, he uttered a "shush" sound and put his finger across my mouth. "What are you doing?" he said. "You've got this all wrong. This is a love story. You need to reach out, touch me, and take care of me."

Huh? I stepped away from the finger and looked at the script again. Did I miss something? Perhaps I *was* wrong. After all, he did graduate from That Prestigious Acting School, and he must know his stuff. I reread the dialogue. The male and female anchors were having an argument on air while reading the news, taking swipes at each other like, "Why Bob, you old gasbag ..." and "Ginny, you ignorant slut." It was almost a word-for-word rip-off of an old *Saturday Night Live* sketch. Even though I was terrible at confrontations at that time in my life, I was able to meekly say "Uh, no. I'm pretty sure it's a, uh, comedy sketch."

"*Cleahly*" he said in a faux British accent, the kind that some American actors put on when they want to show off how talented they are, "you *hahve* no idea about script analysis. I think it best that we stop rehearsing and just *perfohm* the scene. You'll find out I was right."

"Um, okay," I said. "I guess we'll find out."

When it was our turn to do our scene, we were just a few lines into it when the casting director held up his hand and said, "Stop! What are you doing?" Dick smiled and looked at me.

"No, *you*," he said pointing at Dick. "What are *you* doing? Don't you know this is a comedy sketch? You've got the tone all wrong. *NEXT!*"

The lesson I've never forgotten (besides don't be a Dick to a fellow actor) is, no matter how brilliant your technique or illustrious your training might be, if you do not understand the tone of what you're auditioning for, it's a missed opportunity. An actor who reads for a Nickelodeon comedy like an audition for *Hamlet* will be shown the door.

So, how do you define tone? It's an insanely huge topic encompassing many different types of acting styles according to the category of the script. It can be the tone of a genre (e.g., horror, action, romantic comedy); a distinctive writer's style (Aaron Sorkin, Tina Fey); a director's style (Quentin Tarantino, Wes Anderson); or the tone of a particular show (*Gilmore Girls, The Walking Dead*). Knowing tone informs how you approach a script, what kinds of character choices you make, even technical adjustments like vocal volume, pace of your dialogue, and body language. Your audition for a zany TV comedy will likely call for bigger, broader acting choices than an intimate Steven Soderbergh film.

We will take a much deeper dive into tone in Part Three, but because the goal is getting you on your feet for an audition *now*, here are some simple things you can do today:

- If you have an audition for an existing TV show, make sure you've watched at least one episode. If you aren't able to find an entire episode, there usually are trailers or snippets available on the web. This is essential!

- Pay attention to the pace and rhythm of the dialogue. Is it brisk and snappy or more leisurely and naturalistic? Another way to frame this is—overall, does it remind you more of your Personal Scene or your Everyday Scene? This can be true of either comedy or drama.

- If it's a dramatic show, are there glimmers of humor? One of the biggest mistakes actors make is treating all dramatic material as Serious with a capital S. Many great dramatic shows have a sense of irony, however subtle, and the smart actors are able to recognize it. For some examples, start by watching *Succession*, *Justified*, *The Newsroom*, and *The Resident*. See if your script has any opportunity for irony or a lighter moment.

- If this is a new show with no existing video, pay attention to as many details as possible when you get the audition information, also known as the breakdown. Sometimes it will clearly state "half-hour comedy" or "episodic drama." This info usually includes the show creators; look up their past credits—they usually indicate the type of shows they've produced in the past. You might even get a really helpful hint, like "think of Phoebe on *Friends*," to steer you in the right direction.

- If your audition is for a film, there usually is no preexisting footage unless it's part of a franchise, like the Marvel movies. Follow the steps above for as many clues to the tone as possible. An oversimplified rule of thumb is: if it's an indie (independent film), it's usually more about relationships and is slower paced; if it's an action film, the pace is more driven.

- If your audition is live in the casting director's office—*ask*! The casting director is your ally and wants you to succeed—that makes their job so much easier. By asking a simple question about tone for my audition for the film *American Zombie*, I realized my prepared audition was completely off, and I recalibrated my choices on the spot, which resulted in booking the role.

- For theater auditions, your best ally is the director. Again, make sure to ask if you're at all unsure about the tone—they will be eager to share their vision with you. Even if you're auditioning for material by well-known playwrights like Tennessee Williams, David Mamet, or Shakespeare, don't assume you're doing a carbon copy of past performances. The director may have a fresh take on classic material.

I want you to become an expert on tone, to be able to pick up any script and recognize how to approach it successfully. That is one of the hallmarks of an Essential Actor.

ESSENTIAL ACTOR TAKEAWAYS

- For scripted material demanding an emotional connection, use the Personal Scene as your baseline tool to connect.
- Always identify the Hot Person(s) in your scene in order for you to discover your organic behavior with other characters.
- If a scene is more about a situation than a relationship, find your real-life corresponding Hot Situation.
- If there is a confrontation with another character, use the tools in the Hot Person Confrontation exercise.
- If the scene requires a more naturalistic, ordinary approach, use your Everyday Scene mode as your starting point.
- If your character is unable or unwilling to speak their truth during a moment in a scene, play with the Cover tool to add another layer to your work. Remember, the camera can read your thoughts!
- *Always* know the tone of the material you're auditioning for. That will give you an edge in booking the role.

PART TWO

THE PASSIONATE ACTOR

An actor must interpret life and in order to do so must be willing to accept all the experiences life has to offer. In fact, he must seek out more of life than life puts at his feet.

—James Dean

I NEED

He who has a why can endure any how.
—Frederick Nietzsche

The main characters in both comedy and drama have an objective: the thing that they want to attain or the goal they are attempting to achieve. This goal arises from a desperate need, and we the audience root them on their journey as we watch them overcome the obstacles on the way to what may or may not be a successful outcome.

When you are cast in a play, TV show, or film, or are doing a scene in class, your job as an actor is to tell your character's story, and to do that, you need to determine what your character desperately needs, otherwise known as their objective. Common objectives revolve around the themes of finding love, acquiring status or power, protecting loved ones, surviving trauma, overcoming illness, or escaping death.

When I was a beginning actor, I struggled with this concept, but it's actually not so hard to figure out. Sum up in a sentence or two what your character is trying to accomplish. A big hint is to not only pay attention to the dialogue but observe their behavior. Do they say they're not interested in love but show up at a singles bar every night? And at the end of the story, is she elected president? Did he survive his ordeal on the desert island? Now that you know your character's goal, that will inform the choices you make as you start to work on the material.

Matthew McConaughey's character, Ron Woodroof, in *Dallas Buyers Club* is diagnosed with AIDS and is told he has thirty days to live. He bypasses the death sentence of the current medical establishment and finds alternative drug therapy which he first uses for his own survival but then becomes the provider of life-prolonging drugs to other AIDS patients. He *needed* to survive, and in so doing, found his humanity in helping others as well.

Leonardo DiCaprio's character, Hugh Glass, in *The Revenant* is not only left for dead after a bear attack in the frontier winter of 1823, he witnesses the murder of his son by his former hunting team. He almost literally rises from the dead in order to track down his betrayers. He *needed* to survive and travel a great distance in order to avenge his abandonment and his son's murder.

Eddie Redmayne's portrayal of the real-life Stephen Hawking in *The Theory of Everything* was a dramatization of Hawking as a promising college student being stricken with ALS (amyotrophic lateral sclerosis) and how he *needed* to overcome the devastating effects of the disease in order to fulfill his destiny as one of our greatest astrophysicists.

In *Room*, Brie Larson's character, Joy Newsome, desperately *needed* to escape the shed where she had been raped, impregnated, and imprisoned for seven years, in order to be reunited with her family and save her son's life.

In *Bridesmaids*, Kristen Wiig's character, Annie, feels abandoned by everything she loves: her about-to-be-married best friend Lillian, her failed business as a baker, and her heel of a "boyfriend." Her *need* for love and acceptance fuels her desperate actions and makes for great comedy.

When you read a script, you may find your character's life resembles your own and may instantly relate to their journey. But if you're cast in a movie about survival and you've never had to survive, how is that a real scenario for you? How do you, as an actor, truthfully go about personalizing the objective of surviving under dire circumstances if you've never done so before?

What if you've never had AIDS, or a life-threatening disease, or were never attacked by a bear? What if you've never been on the brink of bankruptcy or suffered any loss? What if you're no longer actively searching for love, happy to wake up every morning to the snoring lump next to you?

If you aren't able to make the character objective personally meaningful to you, you can analyze and discuss it all day long, but it becomes an *intellectual idea*. And you cannot *act* an *intellectual idea*. That's the formula for a wooden, disconnected performance.

You can use your imagination in a hypothetical scenario, as in, "What if I was abducted and thought I couldn't see my family for the rest of my life?" (Referred to in Key Terms as What If or the Magic If.) Actors need to be able to use their imagination because, after all, this is make-believe. But even the most fertile imaginations can go cold—at an audition, on a set, or other high-stress situations.

I wanted to find a reliable tool that would provide a strong connection and a way of personalization that would work for my actors every time.

After a recent birthday, I started reflecting upon my life. The goals and dreams that drove me years earlier were still unfulfilled. Where was my TV series or juicy film role? I had just had a callback for a big studio movie with a major star that I desperately wanted and didn't get. That was painful, and it affected me more than usual. I thought, *I have more birthdays in my rearview mirror than up ahead. What the hell has my life amounted to?*

I began to pace and started asking myself, right now, what do I need? I repeated over and over again, "I *need* ... I *need*," with both hands placed firmly over my heart and waited until something came to me.

The answer bubbled into my consciousness like the little triangle in a Magic 8 Ball. I became aware of a great need that I hadn't been in touch with: to be remembered for something significant before I died. I had thought years ago I might write a book one day, and I didn't want the discoveries I've made in my acting classes to die with me. I suddenly needed to write it—to create a legacy of my life's work. This need was so immediate and painful that it brought tears to my eyes, and yet it was exciting and made me feel alive. It shook me out of complacency and gave me a new focus. I had found my personal objective, my I Need. It didn't matter if my friends and family reacted by calling that ridiculous; of course, according to them, my life meant something. But this was *my truth* that resonated with *me*, and that's all that mattered.

If I had done this self-exploration exercise at other times in my life, the answer would have been different. In grammar school, my I Need would have been acceptance by the other students. In my teens, my I Need would have been for my mother to stop drinking and be available to me. In my single years, my I Need would be to find my soulmate. The I Need can change or stay the same your entire life. The key is to be in touch with it.

In your acting work, when you are in touch with your personal objective, it becomes a way for you to align with your character's objective. You may not relate to the desperate need to survive on a desert island, but you may be able to relate to desperately needing the love of a parent. *Getting in touch with what you* need *is your bridge to relating to what your character* needs. It will become a tool you use and part of your engine that drives you when you do scene work.

What you need is what you need. This is not for anyone else to judge or for you to be ashamed or self-conscious about. You don't need to explain or justify it to anyone. It may be in the moment—what you need *right now*: "I Need to get to the airport on time." It may be about a relationship: "I Need my father to love me." It may be existential: "I Need to find my life's purpose."

If you're lucky enough to be a parent, you already have a built-in I Need. From the moment your child was born, you had another human being to take care of, who was dependent upon you for survival. Built into our DNA is our need to keep our offspring safe and alive. If I have an actor in class who is disconnected, stiff, or just shy, I can usually ignite their passion just by using their I Need with their children in whatever form it takes and whatever stage their relationship is in.

It's more than likely you had a taste of your personal objective in your Personal Scene or in your Hot Person exercise. The I Need exercise is a more direct conduit and sheds light on your deepest longing. Self-help groups commonly say that we humans have a hole that we're looking to fill—in other words "I NEED" in capital letters—which can lead some to drug or alcohol abuse or other compulsive behavior. As artists we can use that hole for our art, and how lucky we are for it.

I NEED EXERCISE #1

There is more than one way to fulfill this exercise. You can do it alone, with a partner in class, or both. I find the class version particularly powerful because it requires you to look into another human being's eyes and ask for what you need, which for some of us may be difficult at first but is ultimately extremely empowering.

Step One: Walk around the room with your hands placed over your heart, your solar plexus, or both, and start saying, "I Need" out loud. Say it over and over again until something comes to you. You will know when you have a truthful connection to what your I Need is because you will feel it in your solar plexus or any other part of your body where you experience connection.

Whatever comes up, *don't judge it*. Welcome your I Need and guarantee its safety in your work as an artist. After doing the exercise, no one but you ever needs to know what it is.

Remember, this is not about what you *want* but what you *need*. Right now, I *want* a donut. But I *need* acknowledgment. I *need* to finish this book in order to pass along a lasting legacy about my classes. I *need* to make a difference in people's lives. *Want* can be a passing fancy or a temporary fixation. *Need* goes much deeper into our soul's desires.

If you are in a class, you can do Step One either walking around in the space or quietly sitting alone. There is no need to talk to other students; this is your private time.

Step Two: When you have identified your I Need, select another human being from the class and sit in chairs across from each other. If your I Need is about a relationship, you may want to choose someone who resembles that person in your life.

You will now say your I Need to the other human. Keep it short and to the point, for example, "I Need you to love me." Say it over and over again. Say it and be aware of your connection. This may take several minutes.

(If your I Need is extremely personal and you don't want to share it publicly, I have suggested the student simply say, "I Need *it*." Even though I believe saying your I Need out loud is empowering, as long as you are aware and connected, this is an acceptable alternative.)

> BIG NOTE: The other human being must sit impassively, making eye contact and receive your "I Need." They must not smile, nod, or do anything but listen to you while you are communicating your "I Need." **This is very important!**

When, and only when, you are fully connected to your I Need, and the other human *feels* that connection, they may nod, say yes, and "give" it to you.

The first time we did this exercise in class, there wasn't a dry eye in the house.

Even my most experienced actors, who had up to that point been in touch with their emotional life and their vulnerability, reached another level of connection and truth.

Some examples of I Need that happened in class:

My student Dave talking to his alcoholism: "*I need* to walk away from you. I *need* to not be controlled by you."

Marissa talking to her son: "*I need* you to respect me."

My student Sid, approaching age fifty and about to be a first-time parent: "*I need* more time. *I need* to live a long life to spend as much time as possible with you."

My student Mabel, dealing with the realities of aging: "*I need* to be independent. *I need* to never be put away in assisted living."

My student Jeri talking to her mother, who was recently diagnosed with cancer: "*I need* you to stay alive."

My student Elliot talking to his ex: "*I need* you to feel the pain you inflicted upon me. *I need* you to be hurt the way you hurt me."

My student Ted talking to his mother: "*I need* you to support me in my acting career. *I need* you to stop controlling me and let me be who I am."

But the most common theme, often with a distant parent, child, or spouse, is "*I need* you to love me."

Sometimes this exercise takes some coaching. Rather than focusing on the I Need, some students will meander into a story and explanations. This is a defense mechanism of bypassing the gut connection and getting into the intellect. Or sometimes it's just an angry vent, another defense mechanism. For example:

"*I need* you to pay attention to me. Because we've been together for ten years. Because ten years is a long time. Because Mary's been married for ten years, and her husband talks to her. Because her husband is nice. Because he's happy. Because he has a job. And you don't have a job. Because you're lazy ..."

When an actor is going on a rambling story, I will gently coach them back to the nut of their I Need. In the example above, if an actor is detoured by the "because," I will interject, "*I need* you to see me," or even better and usually more truthful, "*I need* you to love me," and have them repeat it several times. Almost always, that gets them back to their core connection. If they stray again, they are gently led back.

Some actors feel an explanation is necessary—the "becauses" for their I Need—but it's not. I Need is at its best when it's one or at the most two phrases. It's more powerful when the same phrase is spoken over and over again. That's the best way for this to leave your *intellect* and get into your *gut*.

"I need you to love me" is a universal I Need that most of us have experienced in our lives. I don't think it's an accident that so many of us end up in an acting class because of a difficult relationship with a parent, feelings of loss of love or friendship. If you are having trouble finding your I Need or are in a transitional period where your former I Need has lost its power, sit across from another human being and simply say, "I *need* you to love me." You may have a Hot Person in mind, but even if you don't, say it over and over again, making eye contact with that person. I won't even attempt to go into a psychological explanation, but there's something about asking another human being to love us that connects us to our humanity and vulnerability. It's a core personal objective that all of us have.

I Need exercise #2 — Hot Person Intervention

The first I Need exercise gets you in touch with your personal objective—what you need right now, which most of the time involves love or approval from another human being.

This particular exercise is about saving another human being, focusing on someone who needs your help. You will choose a Hot Person in your life—someone who's in trouble, who is self-destructive, depressed, or on the wrong path. Someone you're in danger of losing, and if so, would be a devastating loss.

You will choose a fellow actor to represent this person and sit in chairs facing each other. Take in their facial expression and make deep eye contact. Now, you will talk to them, unscripted, from your heart. I suggest you use the phrase "I *need* you to ..." often. Just like your I Need, keep it short and simple and repeat the same phrase several times if you have to.

Example: "I *need* you to get sober. I *need* you to get sober. Please get sober. Your drinking has hurt me terribly. I *need* you to stop. Please, I *need* you to stop drinking. I *need* you to get sober."

You will use your powers of love, persuasion, logic, or even anger to convince this person to stop their behavior and get them back on the right path. Make one of your objectives to connect to them emotionally and to change the expression in their eyes. The one thing you may not do is touch the other person.

Like the I Need Exercise #1, the other actor must sit impassively until they feel you have achieved the objective, at which time they will nod, acknowledging your success.

This exercise has multiple purposes. One is getting in touch with the part of you that wants to effect change, particularly with a significant human being in your own life. Many times, this is in alignment with a character's heroic objective of saving other people that you may have a chance to play in your career.

The other is taking note of the tactics—or actions—you used. After you're finished, you, your teacher, and fellow classmates can analyze what you did and translate it into active verbs. Did you beg, implore, demand, throw a tantrum, connect, speak heart to heart, appeal, use logic, love, tenderness, understanding? And of these tactics or actions, which had the most success? This will also be helpful in the future, to isolate a particular beat or moment and use a similar action in order to achieve the objective. I also explore this in Part Three but it's useful for you to have a taste of it now.

I Need exercise #3 — Mantra

(I was introduced to the Mantra concept while studying improvisation with Lisa Frederickson at Impro Theatre in Los Angeles. She graciously gave her blessing to share this wonderful exercise. Thanks, Lisa!)

The Mantra is a secret statement known only to the actor, for example, "I've got to get out of here" or "I'm in love with you," and it informs everything from their behavior to the pace of the scene. This exercise is a great foundation for an improvised scene, and I think it translates brilliantly when working with scripted material. Use this mini-scene as an example:

ACTOR 1
I'm glad you're here.

ACTOR 2
I'm glad to be here.

ACTOR 1
I don't have much time.
But I really need a drink.

ACTOR 2
I thought you stopped drinking.

ACTOR 1
I don't mean a drink drink.
Just a drink.

ACTOR 2
Actually, I'd like a drink drink.

ACTOR 1
I knew you'd say that.

Like the Hot Person mini-scene, this mini-scene has no particular context. But if the setting is two exes meeting at a restaurant, Actor 1's Mantra could be "I need you back." It could also be "I need you to apologize to me," or "I need you to suffer"—all according to the given circumstances. Just by committing to the Mantra, it could help you find a core connection, or what is sometimes known as the "spine" of the scene. Note also how the Mantra creates subtext, adding dimension to the scene.

My student Jon Paul Allyn recently booked the major studio movie *The Menu*, which is currently in production as of this writing. The story revolves around the gourmet restaurant industry, where the most ridiculous ingredients are peddled at exorbitant prices. His Mantra for his audition was, "I want to have sex with this food." Choosing this Mantra gave his acting work an irresistible subtext, which resulted in booking a juicy supporting role.

Try these Mantras according to the given circumstances:

For scenes requiring urgency:

- "I don't have time!"
- "I need to get out now!"
- "I'm in big trouble!"

For scenes requiring an emotional connection or a relationship:

- "I love you."
- "I want you to be happy."
- "I need you to love me."

For scenes requiring you to be higher status:

- "I'm better than you."
- "I feel sorry for you."
- "I know everything."

For scenes requiring confrontation:

- "You will not get away with this."
- "I will prove you wrong."
- "I will destroy you."

Other mantras:

- "I feel so awkward."
- "I think you are so hot."
- "I don't trust you."
- "I am fascinated by you."

The next time you work on a scene, ask yourself, "What would my character's mantra be?" and you'll start coming up with your own.

***

Getting in touch with your personal objective or I Need may even transform you for the better. If your newly found I Need is about fixing a relationship, improving your career, or owning your feelings of powerlessness or despair, it can rack focus on that area in your life. Self-awareness not only makes you a better actor, but it's the first step for positive change. One of my actors admitted he had been treading water and was now committed to his life's dream of directing a movie. Another left an unhappy marriage. I wrote this book. You now can choose if you want to take additional steps to get what you need. It gives you the power to bring your full heart and commitment to everything you do—in acting and in life.

I BELIEVE

Integrate what you believe in every single area of your life. Take your heart to work and ask the most and best of everybody else, too.
—Meryl Streep

Many of my favorite moments on film are the Big Speeches that take place during a climactic scene where the character galvanizes the audience in order to inspire, demand results, or win their cause. Some examples are Al Pacino's courtroom speech in *Scent of a Woman*, Julia Roberts's confrontation with the PG&E executives in *Erin Brockovich*, George C. Scott's opening address to his troops in *Patton*, R. Lee Ermey's rant in the beginning of *Full Metal Jacket*, Kelly McGillis's appeal to the jury in *The Accused*, Mark Ruffalo's tirade in *Spotlight*, Denzel Washington's sermon in *Malcolm X*, Jack Nicholson's outburst in *A Few Good Men*, and so many others. These moments make a movie memorable and win awards for the actors lucky enough to be given such powerful words.

One day in class, my student Patrice was doing a scene with one of these climactic speeches. During the speech, Patrice turned away from the audience and started mumbling. We were only a few feet away from her but could barely hear her.

I stopped the scene and asked, "Patrice, what do you believe?"

She paused and swallowed hard. "What do you mean?"

"What do you strongly believe in? What do you stand for? What gets your guts boiling? If there was one thing that you could change in this world and get *us* to believe, what would it be?"

She paused and turned bright red. "I don't know."

"You really don't know, or you don't want to say?"

Her eyes filled with tears. It's not my goal to make my students cry, but in this moment, I knew I was getting close to a breakthrough.

"I don't know. I don't know what I believe in." More tears.

"Let me take a guess," I said. "You were raised in an environment where it wasn't okay to say what you felt or what you believed."

More tears. This was painful but such a pivotal moment.

Very softly. "Yes. That's right."

I could relate to Patrice's emotional response. When I was growing up, many times I was demeaned, ridiculed, or even punished for expressing an opinion that didn't fall into line with my family's way of thinking. And, no surprise, my early acting work suffered because of it.

This moment in class crystallized something I'd been aware of for a long time; I just hadn't been able to articulate it clearly until watching Patrice's struggle. That it's vitally important for an actor to not only be in touch with what they strongly believe; they must be able to express it fearlessly and unapologetically. To be able to do that is to get in touch with our power, which we use as our engine to carry us through many types of scenes or connect to a character. That was the pivotal moment when I Believe became an indispensable exercise in my studio.

If you were to do an internet search for "best inspirational TV and film monologues," you will find a multitude of I Believe moments. These are the moments when a character is using their power of conviction or sense of moral outrage to convince, persuade, inspire, or motivate another character or characters to come to their way of thinking or take action to forward their cause. They are proselytizing to get a result and effect change. Find an episode of the original *Law & Order* series, and watch one of Sam Waterston's jury summations to see an I Believe moment at its finest.

I Believe isn't just for dramatic moments but serves comedy as well. In fact, great comedies are quite often about people with strong, albeit absurd, beliefs. Think of Dwight Schrute in *The Office* ("Bread is the paper of the food industry. You write your sandwich on it.") or Ron Burgundy in *Anchorman* ("They named it Sahn Di-ahgo, which of course in German means, 'Whale's Vagina'"). As Megan, Melissa McCarthy's motivational speech to Kristen Wiig's Annie in *Bridesmaids* is an instant classic and is a great example of an actor in an I Believe moment. ("I'm life, Annie, and I'm biting you in the ass!")

You can use the I Believe exercise to connect to a speech, a character, or a tone of a script. It especially comes in handy when you can't personally relate to the material. My friend Paul is a lifelong liberal and has strong opinions about economic inequality. He took one of my Los Angeles workshops where we did the I Believe exercise. In the second part of the exercise, I handed him the "Greed is good" monologue from *Wall Street*. You couldn't find material more diametrically opposed to the actor's personal beliefs, and yet he found such a strong connection, I hid my purse when he was finished.

In order to rise to the level that this material demands, an actor must be in touch with their personal beliefs and the *issues that get them connected to their gut*. You may believe that McDonald's should serve breakfast all day long, or chocolate is a better flavor than vanilla, or your garden gnome moves while you're not looking, but I encourage you to go deeper. Usually when a student gravitates toward the trivial, they're almost always hiding a deeper truth. You must find the *big ideas* that emanate from the deepest part of your soul and are about your conviction of how to effect change for the better. If nothing comes to mind, start with the phrase, "The world would be a better place if ..."

It's important to note that this is *your belief*. When we perform this exercise in class, we are in a judgment-free zone. We've had many beliefs aired—some can be political or contain a world view that may not be ours. This is not about you pandering to an audience for their approval or censoring yourself because we may not agree with you. Who cares what we think! This exercise is all about the actor's connection, not about the content or our opinion about the content.

To be clear, I Believe and any of my other exercises are not about making threats of harm, even imagined, and even though this is about freedom of expression, that would not be tolerated in class. The point is to appeal to our better angels, to effect change for the betterment of mankind, the animal kingdom, the planet. Acting in its highest incarnation can be a force for society's benefit, so let's use our art for the powers of good, not evil.

The I Believe exercise

The I Believe exercise is an improvised monologue that you will ideally perform in front of a group of people. At its best it's an evangelical speech, the purpose being to proselytize and change the worldview of the group so that they ultimately adopt your point of view. If you don't have a group, you can do this exercise solo. You will still benefit from the feeling of connection.

This is better described as a rant than a monologue—the point is not to deliver a perfectly articulated speech but more of a random stream of consciousness. It's helpful to pace about the stage, rather than standing in one spot. It takes away your self-consciousness about your words and gets you more connected to your gut. The result usually is more eloquent, electric, and impassioned than a well-planned speech.

The rant begins and ends with "I Believe." Here's an example of one of my I Believes that I improvised for a class demonstration.

I Believe people shouldn't be allowed to hunt and kill endangered animals for trophies. Especially elephants, who are sentient, intelligent creatures who have strong family units, who mourn their dead. I saw a picture of a mother elephant who was killed while she was grazing with her baby—the photo showed her bloodied body on the ground with half-eaten grass in her mouth while the baby stood there crying. I Believe that's a disgusting waste of life and it's immoral. It was heartbreaking. We are losing these wonderful creatures to poachers and hunters who are hunting them not for survival but for their own ego. I Believe this needs to be stopped now, before we cause their extinction. I Believe since we have the power over these creatures, we are obligated to save them, not abuse and slaughter them. I Believe elephants have the right to live, and the hunting should stop now! And that's what I Believe.

After the actor is finished, I ask them where they felt the strongest connection in their body. There has been some variety in responses, but the majority point to the middle area of their torso toward the bottom of their ribcage, which I call the solar plexus or gut connection. (Don't know where this is? Put your hand on your mid-torso and cough softly. You can feel that area activate.) That is the strongest connection there is. It's no coincidence that is also where you have the greatest vocal support, for a fuller, more commanding voice. Ideally during your I Believe moments in scene work going forward, this will be the muscle memory you use every time.

For the second part of the exercise, I hand a monologue to the actor to be read *cold*. (There are links to monologues on my website or find your own on an internet search.) They are instructed to use the gut connection they just established and apply it *immediately* to connect to the script. You'll find that even if you aren't the best cold reader, the connection will carry you through the monologue. The I Believe tool fills up your tank and gives you the fuel you need to carry you through the material.

COLD READING TIPS — With a scene or monologue, practice the "Grab and Deliver" technique. Grab a line off the page and while making eye contact with the audience or your scene partner, deliver the line. Try to keep eye contact for the entire line that you grabbed from the page, but at least **land** the last word with the listener before going back to the page for the next line.

This is easier with dialogue that has one or two lines per exchange and trickier with a monologue, especially if the monologue has long sentences. For example, in Lt. Aldo Raine's famous monologue from the movie *Inglorious Basterds*, the sentence "Now, I don't know about y'all, but I sure as hell didn't come down from the goddamn Smoky Mountains, cross five thousand miles of water, fight my way through half of Sicily and jump out of a fuckin' air-o-plane to teach the Nazis lessons in humanity" is too long for most people to remember with one glance. In that case, break it up into sections.

(Glance at page, grab the first part of the long sentence, make eye contact with audience or scene partners, deliver): "Now I don't know about y'all, (glance, grab, eye contact, deliver) but I sure as hell didn't come down from the goddamn Smoky Mountains (glance, grab, eye contact, deliver) cross five thousand miles of water, fight my way through half of Sicily (glance, grab, eye contact, deliver) and jump out of a fucking air-o-plane to teach the Nazis lessons in humanity."

Once again, it's very important that you land the last word of each sentence on a human being's face before you go back to the page. Don't worry, the next line will still be there. After a while you will be able to grab bigger chunks of a long sentence. The more you practice this technique, the easier it gets. (I also have a video showing this technique on my website.)

Sometimes one run-through is all we need. If I feel the actor lost a little connection between the I Believe and the scripted monologue, I'll have them read it again but to imagine their audience as the group they most need to appeal to. For example, the elephant monologue could be delivered to a group of hunters. You may feel righteous anger and moral outrage, but your objective is to get them on your side, not to yell or berate. Remember, your job is to use your passion to appeal, to persuade in order to effect change.

Note: Even though most of the time we see I Believe produce instant fireworks in an actor, every now and then, some actors can find this exercise extremely difficult. It could be all the reasons I mentioned above—having been shamed, punished, demeaned, usually by one's family or peers. It could be inherent shyness. It could be age—this is quite often easier for older people than younger. If you're having difficulty expressing your opinions or coming up with your I Believe, try the advocate approach where you're speaking on behalf of a group who can't defend themselves, like small animals, children, etc. And if something still isn't coming up, I highly suggest you do some soul searching. Look at the current events around you and in the world and determine how you feel about them. Finding your I Believe will not only make you a better actor, it will make you a better human being.

This is one of my favorite exercises because we not only see instant results but some riveting performances. And if the performances are riveting with material you've just picked up for a cold read, imagine what could happen if you had an hour, an afternoon, a day to work on a script. This is a powerful tool for you to do excellent, truthful work, quickly and effectively prepare for auditions, and be well on your way to a career working in TV and film.

THE "IT FUCKING PISSES ME OFF WHEN ..." EXERCISE

There are moments when a script calls for real anger. Even though anger can be a component of I Believe, this one cuts to the chase. Start by pacing and saying out loud "It fucking pisses me off when ..." and complete the sentence. If nothing comes to you, keep saying it until something does. And when it does, continue your rant until you are in a state of full-blown pissed-offedness.

Now that you have that connection, do a web search or go to my website to find links to scripts where you can try this out. It works for either comedy or drama—for comedy I suggest the Felix/Oscar confrontations in *The Odd Couple* and for a dramatic tone the wonderful climactic scene in *A Marriage Story*. This is similar to the Hot Person Confrontation, but with even more heat.

***

Here's what I believe right now. I believe every actor becomes a better actor with the I Believe exercise. I believe you will find your voice and your passion, even if you weren't aware of it before. I believe you can now connect to scripts more deeply than ever before. I believe this exercise can get you closer to achieving your dreams.

And that's what I believe.

MEMORY

Hamlet: Horatio! My father!—methinks I see my father!
Horatio: Where, my lord?
Hamlet: In my mind's eye, Horatio.
—William Shakespeare, *Hamlet*

What is happening with you right now? Is your mind starting to drift? Are you reliving the first bite of your pancakes earlier today? Are you stewing that your spouse didn't pay the credit card bill or replaying the sex dream about your crazy ex? Maybe your mind is drifting to a deeper place—a recent loss, a rift with a friend. Worries about debt or a troubled relationship.

That's natural. Human beings tend to be preoccupied by past events, even while reading an incredibly ingenious and compelling book. No offense taken.

And what happens when the thoughts of past events, relationships, or dreams preoccupy you? Go to one of them right now. To make it easy, just go back to breakfast. Do you see it? Let's say you made pancakes. Do you see them on the griddle? Are you watching yourself getting the butter out of the refrigerator, the syrup out of the cupboard, a plate out of the dishwasher? Damn, you forgot to set the dishwasher—so then you quickly rinsed the plate off in the sink. You dried it off. You grabbed a spatula, loaded the plate with pancakes, applied the butter, drowned them in syrup. Sat down at the table. Picked up a fork. Started to eat.

Notice that I used the word "see." If you were to tell me the story of today's breakfast, you would do so not by reciting the micro-events like a memorized list, *but by describing these images as if you were watching the video playback. You're seeing images as you tell the story.* Your other senses are fired up as well: smell, taste, even touch. (As I'm writing this book, my mouth is watering from the memory of past pancake orgies.)

Think of your most recent delicious meal, and feel how many senses come into play. Think about the first time you fell in love. Think about your last argument. Now notice how vivid these events become as you replay them, how clearly you see them, and how they stir up the same emotions you felt at the time. Sometimes the emotions stay just as raw years later or become muted with age.

We live a lot of life *not* being in the present moment. We mull, we reflect, we daydream, we tell funny stories, we recount details of events ranging from mundane to earth-shattering. And when we relive these experiences—we see, smell, taste, touch, and have emotional recall as if we were transported back to the moment.

Because these moments are also common in scripts, the Memory tool is an important tool to use. Just as in real life, characters quite often talk about something or someone that took place in the past, whether they're speaking about having just ordered room service a moment ago or recalling a tragic loss of a lover a lifetime ago. As an actor, you'll notice these moments are loaded into almost every script you work on. And every time your character mentions anything not happening in the present moment—*you must always have the images in your head of that person, thing, or event, even if it's just a passing reference.* That is the Memory tool.

I started doing the Memory exercises in class when I realized how many moments in scripts demanded a recall of some sort, even something as small as this example.

OFFICE WORKER 1
Hey, any donuts left?

OFFICE WORKER 2
Oh, sorry — I just threw the last one out.

When we do scene critiques in class, we not only talk about Hot Persons, I Need, and all of the bigger concepts, but we also talk about the details. Like those donuts. Did you see them, Office Worker 1? What did they look like? Where did you throw that last one out, Office Worker 2? It takes very little imagination to have a recall of throwing an item of food out—it's something we do every day. (This is obviously a fantasy sequence because only a fool would throw out a perfectly good donut.) But if you're Office Worker 2, we will see a difference between the actor who has no image of this event and the actor who does. It may manifest as an involuntary eye movement, indicating the direction of the trash can. Or there may be no movement at all. In any case, when you see it, we see it. Little, real, subtle details make an enormous difference in a scene, even as simple as this one. Incorporating these details into your work could be the difference between the actor who books and the one who doesn't get the job.

Remember that subtlety is key. You are not "showing" us this memory to prove what an outstanding actor you are. This memory is for you alone. It's yet another way for you to create the reality that grounds you in the scene.

There are other simple Memory moments, like this typical Ladies-Doing-Lunch scene:

LADY 1
How are you and Ted doing?

LADY 2
Oh, fine, he just got a promotion at work.

If the scene feels empty and unconnected, the questions usually are—who is Ted (Hot Person) to both ladies, and for Lady 2—what is the image in her head representing the promotion?

With the information we have from these two lines, it doesn't appear as if the promotion is a big lottery win, just a nice bump. So you, the actor, simply think about a nice recent bump in your life. A little check in the mail? A finished house project? Joined a gym? It doesn't matter what it is. What's important is to find something that fits the mood of the scene and to see that image when you are having the conversation.

Here's the thing. It doesn't have to be a big moment, or a big memory. It doesn't have to be a cinematic marvel in your head. *It just has to be something specific.* When you see something specific, the moment will feel real and full. After a while, filling in these little Memory moments will become reflexive for you.

There are entire scripts devoted to memories. *The Glass Menagerie* by Tennessee Williams is described as "a memory play" retold by the main character Tom Wingfield. But Memory moments are sprinkled throughout many dramatic pieces, even if the overall play or movie is about something else entirely. While writing this chapter, I took a break and happened to watch *The Intern*, starring Robert DeNiro and Anne Hathaway, and was struck by how most of their initial conversations involve their memories.

In the scene where the characters Jules and Ben have their first real conversation, Jules finds out that Ben, her seventy-year old intern, worked for forty years in the building where she now has her successful internet clothing company. Ben takes her on a memory tour of what was once a phone book publishing factory: where his office was, where the printing presses were, the day the sycamores were planted in front. It's clear that Ben still sees the office as it once was, and we get emotionally caught up in the pride and nostalgia he feels as he's transported by this vivid memory.

A little later in the movie, as Ben and Jules are relaxing (platonically) on her hotel bed after a false fire alarm evacuation, she asks him about his late wife. He replies, "We met when we were 20. I was 20, she was 19. What was amazing is that she never really changed."

Moments later, Jules shares what Ben already knows—that her husband is cheating on her, which she discovered after reading the texts on his cell phone: "She sent him a photo which is now forever implanted in my brain."

Even though *The Intern* is about the reinvention of Ben's once-lonely life and the friendships and love that he finds as an intern in Jules's company, there are multiple Memory moments in several scenes. If you've seen the movie, you've observed both actors using this tool. Their memories may have been real and personal, or imagined—we'll never know. But DeNiro and Hathaway, who both happen to be Oscar® winners, understand the importance of using Memory to make a script come alive.

Notice that even though these passages contain a character's Memory moments, their purpose isn't self-indulgent or narcissistic. They are in the context of a relationship and an objective. Sharing a memory can serve many purposes—to reveal oneself in order to create a bond of love or friendship, to get comfort, to achieve resolution. A memory is a way for a character to communicate what they need. The Memory tool helps the actor achieve it.

If you were to do an internet search, you would find an overwhelming amount of monologues and other material from plays and movies where a character is in full recall or Memory mode of an event, a relationship, a wish, or a fantasy. These can be several different tones and themes—telling a funny story; describing a traumatic event; a confession; a reporting of an occurrence; a nostalgic portrayal of a relationship, place, or event; a retelling of a dream; or a memory of loss or betrayal.

One of my favorite examples of a character recalling a darkly comedic moment is from the movie *Passion Fish*, where the character Nina tells her actress friends about her experience on her first movie. It starts with her reciting the memorable line, "I didn't ask for the anal probe" and goes on to describe her ridiculous experience on a low-budget movie. How many times have you had a nightmare audition or acting job? As you continue your career, I guarantee you'll have several of these war story–type anecdotes to share with your fellow actors, and they'll be the highlight of your get-togethers.

And on the opposite side of the spectrum—a speech in court from *The Laramie Project* given by Matthew Shepard's father, Dennis, played by Terry Kinney. He starts with this description: "My son Matthew did not look like a winner. He was rather uncoordinated and wore braces from the age of thirteen until the day he died." It's the father's memory of seeing his son die in the hospital after being tortured. The speech then transforms into one of grace by virtue of the father's beautiful memories of stargazing with his son, and his depiction of the love and comfort that surrounded him upon his death. The actor imbues it with grief, moral outrage, and hope. The emotional impact of that monologue is beyond description.

In your acting journey, you will identify these Memory moments, both important and mundane, comic and tragic. Get used to "seeing" every one of them. Sometimes they will impact you emotionally, involving your cast of Hot Persons or Hot Situations. Or sometimes, they'll just be a donut.

Depending on the type of Memory moment in a given script, I've used either my own memories or my imagination or a combination of both. As you continue to work on scripts, I encourage you to find what works for you. There are as many possibilities as there are moments in scripts, and those are the exciting and creative discoveries you will make. In any case, here are some exercises to start building your Memory muscle.

Memory Exercise #1 — Family Remembrance Monologue

Think of a time in your life that you remember fondly—maybe it involves a family member or members, a childhood friend, or someone else with whom you had a warm relationship. Now think about something that they would do on a regular basis—an endearing quirky habit or just a ritual they enjoyed—either involving you or just something you observed. This should not be a big thing or a heavy emotional moment, just a slice of life, ideally also involving a favorite childhood food or beverage.

An example of this type of reminiscence: *I remember every Friday night my father would play a jazz record after dinner, and our family would sit by the fire playing cards. Occasionally my parents would offer us kids a sip of their beer. If my mother drank a little too much, she'd try to teach us kids how to dance the jitterbug, while my father kept rhythm by tapping on the card table. Then he'd stand up and twirl her around, saying, "I'm a damned good dancer for a fat, bald guy," making all of us laugh.*

Now that you've thought of your own warm slice-of-life event, say it out loud, either to another actor or alone. If you can record it, even better. Don't push it or perform it—just tell the story as you remember it.

Whether or not you recorded it, take note of these details: how vividly you saw your images, what your inflections were, how you used your body and your gestures, and how this memory emotionally resonated with you.

Now, using this following script, infuse it with the same muscle memory, inflections, and emotional resonance you created with your own memory.

It was always cold in the city in July, but Mama would never turn the heat up. She said it was a sin to pay for heat in the summer. So, we'd sit and watch television, and even though we were freezing, Mama would feed us ice cream and root beer floats. "Ah, summer food, you only get to eat like this once a year—let's live a little!" And then, when I caught my inevitable cold, she'd say, "Isn't it a shame to be sick indoors when it's such beautiful weather outside?" To this day, I always wear a sweater in July because, you never know ...

Are you allowed to take the circumstances of this script and use your own imagination of the memory, as the character has portrayed it? Absolutely, yes. But the point is for you to notice all the details of your Memory mode when you're recalling your nostalgic event and for you to utilize those details with scripted dialogue.

Memory exercise #2 — comedic story

This exercise requires a group of at least three people to be effective. Think of a funny story that still amuses you, ideally something that happened to you or you witnessed. You may have that story right now in your pocket ready to go. If not, take a moment and think about it. See the images in your head, let them land in your body, and allow them to make you laugh.

Now, tell this story to the group, and don't be afraid to embellish with physical comedy or gestures, facial expressions, and imitations of other characters involved. Make this as full and big as you can, as if you're performing a stand-up routine. Record yourself if possible. Take note of your inflections, body language, emotions, and particularly, how and when you laughed in the retelling of this story.

You can use this same storytelling mode to bring life to written text, even Shakespeare. Here's Puck's speech in *A Midsummer Night's Dream, Act 3, Scene 2*:

My mistress with a monster is in love.
Near to her close and consecrated bower,
While she was in her dull and sleeping hour,
A crew of patches, rude mechanicals,
That work for bread upon Athenian stalls,
Were met together to rehearse a play
Intended for great Theseus' nuptial-day.
The shallowest thick-skin of that barren sort,
Who Pyramus presented, in their sport
Forsook his scene and enter'd in a brake
When I did him at this advantage take,
An ass's nole I fixed on his head:
Anon his Thisbe must be answered,
And forth my mimic comes. When they him spy,
As wild geese that the creeping fowler eye,

Or russet-pated choughs, many in sort,
Rising and cawing at the gun's report,
Sever themselves and madly sweep the sky,
So, at his sight, away his fellows fly;
And, at our stamp, here o'er and o'er one falls;
He murder cries and help from Athens calls.
Their sense thus weak, lost with their fears thus strong,
Made senseless things begin to do them wrong;
For briers and thorns at their apparel snatch;
Some sleeves, some hats, from yielders all things catch.
I led them on in this distracted fear,
And left sweet Pyramus translated there:
When in that moment, so it came to pass,
Titania waked and straightway loved an ass.

The reason for using the Shakespeare text is manyfold. I've seen too many Shakespeare performances treated like Important Oratory Speeches with bad British accents, and the result is lifeless and boring. Shakespeare's writing was written for flesh-and-blood human beings—so start with yourself. This is a heavy-lifting exercise but great training for you to personalize difficult classical language.

Start by translating the Elizabethan English to standard American (or whatever your native language is), so you are clear about the meaning. You can find current Shakespeare translation resources with an internet search. In the above monologue, Puck is recounting to his master Oberon how a spell he cast on Titania resulted in her falling in love with an ass, otherwise known as the character Bottom. (The hapless Bottom was rehearsing a play with his cohorts when Puck changed his head into a donkey head, thereby Titania's beloved ass.) You can use the Memory mode to "see" the events of your comedic story and use that same mode to "see" Titania (his mistress), the rude mechanicals (the bumbling amateurs rehearsing a play) scattering madly when they saw their friend wearing the donkey's head. In our stories, we usually mimic other people—you can do the same thing describing and mocking these other characters. Those are the details that bring Shakespeare and every other script to life.

Memory exercise #3 — memory of personal loss

At some point in our life, we've all experienced a loss of a loved one. Here is an exercise for you to personalize a script about loss—whether it be by death, divorce, desertion, or the end of the relationship or friendship. (If this was the basis of your Personal Scene, you already have a leg up on this exercise.)

Here is the text you will use, Heinrich's monologue from *The Living Hours* by Arnold Schnitzler.

I can remember the day when my mother told me, "Papa has gone away." When he didn't come back, I imagined for a long time that he had died, and I often wept bitterly about it at night. But after a while I met him in the street and with him was that woman for whom he left my mother. I stood inside a doorway so that he might not see me. I, a child, was ashamed in his presence. Yes, I soon understood that my mother was quite free, free as if she had really been widowed. Pardon me, I express myself badly.

Note that the script is not about the literal death of the narrator's father, but it is about the death of their relationship and is therefore a loss. The trap many new actors fall into is to assume this material calls for a self-indulgent, tearful breakdown. An important factor of the Memory tool is to take into account when the memory happened. If the loss happened yesterday, that would have a different impact than if the loss happened twenty years ago. When you read the text of the monologue in this exercise, it's clear that this is a more distant memory, therefore the memory you choose should have a more distant and nostalgic nature, rather than the rawness of a recent loss. If I were to work on this monologue, I might use the sudden death of my father when I was a teenager. At the time it was shocking and heart-rending, but years later, it's evolved into a more wistful remembrance.

Think about a loss you experienced that has some distance to it. Depending on your age, it could be the death of a parent, a childhood friendship that ended, a romantic break-up. Now tell the story of that loss and record it on video if you can. Don't reach for or push an emotion; just tell it as you recall it, and allow the movie of the memory to play in your head. See the story you're telling.

Now, while you're in the same mode, tell your story using the words of the text. When you say, "I often wept bitterly about it at night," keep in mind this is a remembrance of an emotion in the past, not necessarily a cue for tears now. It may affect you emotionally or it may not. The most important thing is to use your own truth.

***

There are so many other types of Memory moments in scripts—this chapter only begins to scratch the surface. You will begin not only identifying Memory moments in scripts but of honing your own technique of bringing them to life. As your memories are uniquely yours and yours alone, in turn your performances will be as well.

PLACE

Locations are characters in my movies. The city is capable of portraying a mood a scene requires.
—Sidney Lumet

If there's one tool you can use consistently in every scene or acting job you do, it's using the setting or Place. Every scene in a TV show, play, or movie happens in an environment—whether it's an apartment, doctor's office, courtroom, the beach, a restaurant, or Mars. As you experienced in your Personal Scene, the place where the event occurred is an important component of that three-dimensional experience. You can use your "where," or your Place, to ground you and connect you to a scene. Sometimes it's all you need.

Place can be an important factor in determining your mode of behavior. You are in a different mode in your bedroom than you are in a hospital ER than you are in the drunk tank. Right now, notice how these suggestions of place affect your inner life:

- Your kitchen
- Your family home where you grew up
- Your office or place of work
- Your dentist's office
- The DMV
- The airport security line
- The beach
- Your favorite coffee shop
- A graveyard

You likely got an immediate image and feeling associated with each of these places. This is an important bit of information to take note of in your journal—it will help you bring a big slice of believability to your acting work, particularly when the place has a direct effect on your state of mind and emotional inner life.

Incorporating Place to connect to the truth of a scene sometimes works apples for apples—your scene may be an Everyday Scene between husband and wife in the kitchen. If so, you can envision your own kitchen to imbue it with the same reality. The scene may occur in your character's workplace, again, using your own place of work where you feel confident and grounded—unless you hate or feel demeaned by your job. Then choose a place where you are the master of your domain.

When the given environment is stressful, affecting your character's state of mind, and if it aligns with your own stressful environments, great. For example, if your character has a meltdown standing in a long line at the DMV and you can personally relate to that, use it. If it doesn't, you can use your own, like the freeway during rush hour, the dentist's chair, or any number of places that push your buttons.

Besides affecting your inner life, using your Place presents possibilities of acting choices you can make, adding texture to your scene work and auditions. We are always looking for the tiny details of human behavior—the things we humans do naturally. For example, if we're in a new environment, we tend to look around with fresh eyes and take note of where we are. The environment can impact our state of mind, whether it's potentially dangerous, exciting, interesting, disgusting, nostalgic, or a myriad of other possibilities. In the first beat of the scene, this new place can affect how we interact with other human beings. And yet, time and again, a student will start a scene or audition and ignore this vital detail.

We recently did a scene in class from *Dexter*, where Dexter's sister, Debra, is meeting her boyfriend on a yacht. She's never been on board this yacht before, and her first line is "Wow, nice place." Being in this new, plush environment could inform her feelings about her lover and her excitement about their rendezvous—which is important, given how the circumstances unfold—that this boyfriend is a serial killer planning to murder her. And yet the actress just walked on stage, without even a glance at her surroundings. It completely took us out of the reality of the scene. After we fixed it by adding that one detail of taking in the luxurious interior upon her entrance, once again we felt like we were eavesdropping on human behavior. It set up her mood of romantic expectations and made it even more devastating when the boyfriend attacks her.

Another example is a scene from *Hung*, where the lead character, Ray, is starting his career as a male prostitute and meeting a prospective client in her hotel room. Entering an unfamiliar hotel room occupied by a stranger you're about to have sex with is a moment that's loaded with emotional possibilities—excitement, arousal, nervousness—and yet the actor simply entered the stage and started talking, completely ignoring the environment and missing the opportunity.

Note that the above scenarios took place in my acting studio, where we have some basic furniture pieces but no elaborate set. This forces the actors to use their imagination and to "see" the details of their surroundings, which is especially valuable training for auditions in a bare room with just a camera and a casting director or camera operator. That sterile audition scenario usually throws a beginning actor. One of the first things I do in a coaching session with a nervous actor is to have them look around and imagine a familiar place of their own where they are at their calmest. I have them describe the walls, paint color and decorations, furnishings, appliances, floor. Then I'll have them look around and describe the surroundings where the scene takes place. It relaxes them almost immediately and puts them into the right mode of behavior. A casting director won't do that—they'll expect you to enter the audition room relaxed and ready to go. You'll be able to do that when you start "seeing" your Place as a second nature.

Almost always, using your Place involves creating the fourth wall (see Key Terms—the space separating the actor from the audience or camera). When the actor looks in that direction, instead of seeing shadowy audience heads or the Teamster eating a donut behind the camera, they "see" the imaginary wall or area that would be there.

In the examples of *Dexter* and *Hung*, I had my students imagine all of the specific details in the yacht and hotel room (polished wood, luxurious furnishings, a view from a window), so that when they looked in the direction of the audience, they "saw" their environment. For any on-camera work, the environment toward and beyond the camera is the fourth wall. If your scene takes place in your kitchen, your fourth wall might be the hallway leading to the dining room. If you've seen a shot where the actor opens a refrigerator and their face is in frame, the camera is smack-dab in the fourth wall, but the actor imagines looking at leftovers. When you get in the habit of using the fourth wall, it becomes your safe place. You create and live in that world and ideally, forget about us. If we're lucky, we will feel like we're eavesdropping.

Place exercise #1 — Beautiful Place

This is an exercise we do in class as a demonstration of how a memory of a happy place or event can change our mood. Even though this is a great bonding exercise to share with a group, you can easily do it alone.

Think of one of the happiest moments of your life. I hope you've had several or at least one. This could be your wedding, the birth of your child, a triumph or accomplishment like winning a sports event, or a standing ovation on stage. It can be a beautiful, peaceful moment you experienced in nature while on a hike or stargazing. It can be observing a beautiful piece of art or at a performance. It can be a Christmas morning in your childhood getting a special gift. Any time in your life when you felt happiest.

Now place yourself back in that setting and visualize every detail of your surroundings. Be specific. Notice colors and smells. In class we say this out loud as if giving a virtual tour, like this example.

It was the opening night of my one-woman show in Hollywood. I can see the theater seats—they were actually rows of benches covered in black material—and the faces of friends sitting in the audience. I see my friend Bill up in the fourth row. I see the red-carpeted steps with the lighting strips on either side of the audience. I see the lighting booth up above. Behind me I see the backdrop with "Andi's Act" painted in glitter. I turn around and see the faces of my back-up singers, Cynthia, Evy, and Shondell, my musicians, and the other characters. (The joke was it really wasn't a one-woman show.) I hear the laughter, and at the curtain call at the end of the show, after a tumultuous rehearsal process where at times the show seemed doomed to certain failure, I take the moment in. I experience the same feeling as I did in that moment, and tears come to my eyes. I am completely happy. It feels as real to me now as it did over twenty-five years ago.

Find your moment, and now, out loud, describe the place where it occurred as precisely as possible. Point out objects, colors, smells, landscape or building details, the other people there. As you're pointing them out, see, smell, feel all of these details fully, and allow them to transport you back to the event. Remember, you are seeing a 360-degree environment, including your fourth wall. Now just take a moment and quietly allow it to affect you. Take your time. If you have been able to do this with a group, we are also seeing the place and event as you've described it and are quietly enjoying it with you.

In other acting methods, most specifically the Stanislavski technique, this is much like the Affective Memory concept. This same process can be used to evoke memories of sadness, trauma, fear, and other emotions. I use it in this exercise specifically for relaxation and happiness. It can put you in a happy, relaxed, content place when you're feeling stressed or uncomfortable. This is a powerful exercise before an audition to calm yourself down. It reminds you that good things have happened in your life and will continue to happen in the future.

Place exercise #2 — your childhood home

This exercise is similar to Exercise #1, but you are specifically using your childhood home. In the same way, either giving a tour out loud or imagining it as a private meditation, you "walk" through the home where you grew up, starting by describing every detail of the outside entrance, walking through the entry, through the living room, kitchen, bedrooms, etc. If you remember your neighborhood, you can take us outside and give us that tour as well.

This exercise has different meanings and outcomes for everyone. For some people it's nostalgic, for others it's painful. If memories of your childhood home were too painful for you, find a place that has warm, nostalgic memories, and do the same exercise, giving a tour with detailed description. Take note and write in your journal the outcome of this exercise for you. It could be a very important emotional tool for future scenes.

Now take this text written by my friend, the wonderful writer Charles Freericks, from his upcoming work *I Can't Believe You Took Me Seriously*. This excerpt recalls his memories of growing up in Paramus, New Jersey. Your objective is to employ the same muscle memory of describing your childhood home to personalize these words. When you "see", "hear", and "smell" the details of what you're describing—the Midland Gulf station, the yelling roosters, the dry cleaning fluid—you will make this Place come alive for your audience.

On Midland Avenue there's a milk and butter store with a wooden box outside. It's got fresh hard rolls and newspapers inside. You pay on the honor system; leave some money in the box. The store's sign says Kenwood Market, but everyone calls it Barney's, after Barney, the owner who died before I ever knew him.

A block closer to Spring Valley Road is Midland Gulf. Robert the owner just hired Ed, a new mechanic. They pump Good Gulf and No-Nox. Ed's going to own the station a decade from now.

Farther east are the Boys Club and Kay Weber School of Dance. But between them is the house with the chickens and roosters that yell at you as you ride by on your bike.

At Forest Avenue is the little shopping center where Harry's Barber Shop's two chairs are reflected smaller and smaller, like Russian dolls, in the infinity mirrors caked with cigarette smoke. Next door is Stone's Sweet Shop. There's a soda fountain, but the stools are piled with boxes of new merchandise and bound magazines. The Stones believe every child is a thief and they watch each one suspiciously.

In front of Stone's there's a card table set up for some politician running for trustee of something.

The first store that faces the other way, towards Forest Avenue, is Paramus Drugs with its perfume of lipsticks and lotions. The pharmacists, the Buechlers, are father and son. The drugstore shares a wall with Fuss-C Cleaner with its perfume of dry-cleaning fluid.

Next over, Trauch's bakery has a ball above the counter with an endless length of string coming out of it that the ladies in pink dresses use to bundle thin cardboard boxes full of butter cookies, and pink sandwich cookies, and thumbprint cookies full of jam. The chill of the bakery grasps hold of Emil's Foodtown too, the grocery store with its saw-dust-covered floors and conveyer belts into the deep basement, where bananas and cat food magically appear.

Charles Freericks ©2022

When you merge the telling of your own nostalgic place with your imagination to describe an environment in any scripted material, you are building a powerful technique to bring richness and magic to all of your performances.

PLACE EXERCISE #3 — BUILD A PLACE

This exercise is not only about seeing your environment, but also seeing and dealing with the objects in the environment. It's just as important that you see those objects as it is seeing the larger Place. This is best done with a group of people.

You will pick a common room or other environment, like a kitchen, bathroom, office, den, etc. The first actor will enter the room, preferably through an imaginary door in order to keep up the illusion that we are seeing all elements of the room, including walls and doors. They will establish and use one object in the room—everything being a "space" object. (Note: in improvisation, everything imagined— furniture, objects, etc.—are called "space" objects. Think in terms of what takes up space, rather than outer space.) For example, if they're entering a bathroom, they may study their face in the "space" mirror of the "space" medicine cabinet, and then open and close the cabinet door. The next actor enters the stage through the same door, looks in the mirror, opens the medicine cabinet, and they may pull out a "space" toothbrush and start brushing their teeth. The third actor does the first two activities and a new one of their own. This continues for as many actors as are playing, and obviously the actors who go up later are the ones who have to remember all of the objects and the activities.

If you're picking up a toothbrush or any other object, it's important to create the space and weight of the object and pick it up and use it as you would a real toothbrush. Some actors will keep their fingers pinched together and use it on their closed mouth. (That's one way to get gingivitis.) The point is to get in the habit of using and feeling the object as realistically as you would in real life.

It's also important to pay attention to the exact location where an object was established. We've had exercises where objects move radically. One actor may establish a refrigerator downstage (toward the audience), and by the end of the exercise, the fridge has migrated all the way upstage (farthest away from the audience). Unless your Place is a haunted house, keep the objects and furnishings where they are. The more closely you observe, the more you will be able to "see" the objects, and they'll stay in their original space.

I saw a production of *American Splendor* on stage in Los Angeles. Besides great performances by Dan Castellaneta and Siobhan Fallon, the most amazing thing about the production was it was done entirely without props or any set pieces, including bar stools or any chairs. They perched on imaginary bar stools, rested their arms on an imaginary bar, and drank out of imaginary glasses. When they put a glass down, they picked it up exactly where they had left it. After a while, the audience could "see" everything, as if it was a completely furnished stage. It was one of the most memorable live performances I've ever witnessed.

Why do this exercise? Strengthening your ability to see objects that aren't there prepares you for on-camera or self-tape auditions, where it's just you, a camera, lights, and a reader. The better your ability to "see" your environment and the objects contained therein, the more grounded your auditions will be.

PLACE EXERCISE #4 — ACTIVITIES IN AN ENVIRONMENT

Like the previous exercise, this one has you working in a mime environment, but you alone are creating all of the elements in it and dealing with them.

I've coached actors for a multitude of taped auditions for working characters, like a bartender. Casting directors discourage using props, however, for a role where your job requires activity, it's very effective to create the environment and do the task that one would do. I've done auditions both ways, either with a minimum of simple props or sometimes without any props at all.

I coached actress Andrea Preisler for one of these roles on *Bloodline*. In our first read-through, we did it without activity. Since she was playing a bartender at an open-air shack in Key West, it just didn't have the relaxed tone that the role required. So, I had her wipe down an imaginary bar counter with a space rag, mime pouring beers from a tap, grab a space glass from an imaginary shelf at her side. All of this while she was engaged in dialogue (aka Walking and Chewing Gum, Part Three) with the main character. Since I was filming her from the top of the chest up—the camera didn't really see the activity, but it showed someone absorbed in what they were doing—and not acting. It worked beautifully; now she looked like an old pro who'd been slinging booze for years. And she booked the job.

For you to prepare yourself for this type of audition, start getting familiar working in an imaginary environment. Experiment now with your own bar. See the counter, grab a (space) rag and start wiping it off. Now see the taps, grab a (space) beer mug and fill it with beer. Put the beer on the counter. See a shelf of liquor bottles behind you, grab one and a (space) shot glass. Fill the glass. Put it on the counter.

You can do this with any environment—a doctor's office, the beach, Disneyland. The point is to start to "see" these imaginary places and the objects associated with them. This skill will ground your auditions and give them a sense of reality. You may not actually do the physical activity—for example, if Andrea was at a live audition, she might not do the action of wiping down an imaginary bar—but her attitude of being preoccupied with her tasks would still carry over. When casting directors and producers see this natural behavior in a script that they've created, it gives them a clear vision of how you would seamlessly fit into their project and make you a top contender for the role.

ACTIONS

Every action needs to be prompted by a motive.
—Leonardo da Vinci

Shortly after moving to St. Petersburg in 2010, I made the decision to start an acting class, despite the fact that I knew very few people and had no established reputation as an acting coach. I had a space rented in the downtown area and my first class date was set—Wednesday, October 6. With two weeks to go, I had three people signed up: a local actress who I had privately coached, a neighbor I met at a backyard barbecue, and a friend of a friend's coworker. Facebook announcements netted zero interest. Even my star turn as host of the relationship-gone-bad TV show *Friends or Lovers* a decade earlier didn't help my cause. (Irony alert: Nobody watched *Friends or Lovers.*)

Although the situation seemed bleak, I'm ridiculously optimistic. My goal was to get a minimum enrollment of ten. My only course of action was to post fliers in local shops surrounding my rental space as a last-ditch effort to drum up more students.

With fliers and tape in hand, I went door to door and tried to engage as many shop owners as possible. It was soon obvious that this group was solidly in the "Never watched *Friends or Lovers*" column and couldn't care less about my acting class or helping me promote it.

I had a very strong I Need (objective): to start my acting class. I also had an enormous obstacle: "Get the hell out of my store!" To overcome this obstacle and achieve my goal, I had to dig deep and use every communication bell and whistle I possessed to get what I wanted. I had to persuade, to engage, to educate, to charm, to plead, to entertain, to ingratiate, to befriend.

What do all of those words have in common? They're active verbs, and they signify the actions I executed to achieve my goal in order to overcome the obstacle in my way. After a long afternoon, most of my fliers were successfully posted, and two weeks later, I had ten students.

On a set, the word "Action!" is used to start the filming of a scene. Action can also mean the given physical activity in a scene, like running after a bus, folding laundry, or pulling a gun on an assailant. In this chapter, Action is a "doing" verb used by one human being to get something from—or offer something to—another human being in order to achieve an objective. The doing verbs usually fit in a "I ... you" sentence (e.g., "I enlighten you." "I threaten you." "I command you."). So, I might say to you: "Buy ten copies of my book for your friends!" using the action "to command." And if my action was effective and got the response I wanted, you're now online ordering the books, and I've achieved my objective. Thanks!

Some acting methods use actions as one of the first steps of scene work, instructing students to determine the scene objective and then assign an action to each line or beat in a script (sometimes called "Actioning") to achieve that objective. The theory of Actioning is it elicits spontaneous behavior from the actor, which in turn provides an emotional connection.

This works well for some people, but when I was a beginning actor, I found this technique extremely difficult. When it came to choosing the actions for a scene before I connected to it in my gut, not only was I completely lost, but I had trouble with the logic of it. In real life, we know what we want to achieve, but we usually don't plan our actions ahead of time! Rather, we live our lives moment to moment, and we don't know the outcome in advance. When I walked into those shops in St. Petersburg, I didn't know if I would be met with success or failure. Every action I used was either spontaneously moving forward after a yes or overcoming the obstacle of a no.

When it comes to scripted scenes, we, the actor, know what the scene's outcome will be, but we have to remember, our character *does not.* For example, if your character is asking a very hot Hot Person out on a date, you've read the scene and you know how it ends. Your first line may be as simple as:

YOUR CHARACTER
Would you like to go out with me?

Now, forget the rest of the script, and just focus on that line. That moment is fraught with uncertainty. What if they say no? What would your Plan B be? There is a universe of possibilities loaded into that one line. Even if you, the actor, know the other character will say yes and you end up getting married on page 100 of the script, your character does not and is waiting in great anticipation for the response.

As I mentioned in Key Terms, each of these lines or moments signifies a Beat. Your character's line above is a beat. The other character's response would be another beat. You've experienced these beats unfolding naturally in some of the previous exercises, particularly the I Need and the Hot Person Intervention, where you were going after something that you desperately needed and yet not necessarily knowing if or when you would get what you wanted. That's how every moment in every scene should be approached, as if the outcome is uncertain.

In order to keep this sense of spontaneity, I start my scene work by identifying the Hot Person, I Need, Personal Scene, or any of the other connection tools and rehearse a "rough draft" of the scene. If there are moments that need more focus, nuance, or connection—like a painter uses highlights and shading, I then use actions to fill in these moments and give them more definition.

Let's use the following scene as an example. It takes place in an arbitration hearing with an abusive ex who used to have power over you, and now you are taking a stand and getting your power back. (Anyone come to mind? Good. You're already connected to both Hot Person and your I Need.)

```
INT. ARBITRATION ROOM - DAY

                         YOU
          I am going to keep the house.

                         THEM
           That's not going to happen.

                         YOU
             You don't have a choice.
          (pushes document across table)
                  Sign this now
               or get ready for a long
                  losing battle.

                         THEM
           Baby, it doesn't have to be
          like this. We can try again.
```

YOU
It's been over for a long time.
I never want to see you again.

If you're using an effective Hot Person, you may have already performed an Oscar® -winning scene in your head. But what if your version is angry and one-note with very little variety? And what if the tone of the scene or the director demands a more contained, nuanced performance? Now, using the same connection you've established as your emotional foundation, try these actions and see how they modify your performance:

YOU
I am going to keep the house.
("*To calm them*"— if you're not sure, think of the opposite of "*to inflame*")

THEM
That's not going to happen.

YOU
You don't have a choice. ("*To taunt them*")
(pushes document across table)
Sign this now
or get ready for a long
losing battle. ("*To caution them*")

THEM
Baby, it doesn't have to be like this.
We can try again.

YOU
It's been over for a long time. ("*To deflate them*") I never want to see you again. ("*To shut down*" or figuratively, "*to close the door.*")

You may have noticed that identifying and committing to those actions brought more definition to your moments. Or if you began the scene with no Hot Person in mind, (which you really shouldn't do, but it happens), you may have found a connection just by the actions alone. If you are on a set and need to do a second, third, fourth, fifteenth take, knowing your actions can help you recreate your performance in a spontaneous way. If you've chosen an action for a particular moment, all you need to do is commit to it, and the moment comes alive.

How do we begin to choose the right actions for a scene? It takes practice and awareness of scene tone and objective. You would choose different actions for confrontational scenes than you would for a romantic scene or a comedy. The first step of making these choices is observing our own actions that we use to achieve our objectives—overcoming the obstacles we face every day.

In life, we embody active verbs without being aware of it. On a first date, we flirt, we intrigue, we seduce. When a loved one is grieving, we comfort, we empathize, we advise. When we are making a sales pitch, we dazzle, we compliment, we persuade. When facing down a threat, we resist, we confront, we attack.

Using the examples above, if we are on a date and my goal is a relationship with you, in the course of the evening, these are the actions I might employ: I flirt with you. I entertain you. I charm you. I seduce you. I impress you. Once again, notice the sentence starts with "I" and ends with "you." I may achieve the goal—or if you have absolutely no taste, I may not. In life, we don't necessarily know the outcome of what we set out to achieve, and yet we take these action steps regardless.

BIG NOTE: Not every effective action fits into the neat starting-with-"I," ending-with-"you" mold.

Some common action phrases I'll use are "To get you to feel my pain," "To get you to take responsibility," "To get you to understand every word I'm saying," "To get you to feel my sarcasm," etc. I also use imagery like "To walk on eggshells" or "To pave the way" in broaching a difficult subject, and figurative images like "To hug," which brings warmth without a physical hug, or "To stab"—to wound or attack another character verbally without physically touching them. I use "To paint a word picture" to get another character enraptured with my vision. In our arbitration scene, I used the figurative "To close the door." These are just a few examples, and in class I come up with similar imagery-type action phrases that help my students refine and focus a particular moment in a scene. When you start playing with these actions, after a while you'll come up with your own.

Now that you're aware of your own actions, work backward from the exercises we've already done, and take note of the actions you did organically. For example, in the Hot Person Mini-Scene (Part One Exercise #2), Hot Person #1 was someone who made you fearful or uncomfortable, which by the way is an obstacle, because the very act of communicating with them is difficult.

YOU
Do you have a moment?

HOT PERSON
Not now, I'm busy.

YOU
I think you really need to listen.

Can you identify the verb/action you employed with your first line? Was it to broach, to tiptoe, to apologize, to pacify? What about your second line? To cajole, to persuade, to beg?

Now you can experiment with adding different actions to experience how they change the scene for you. Try the scene at least twice or more with different verbs—some are suggested in parentheses.

You: Do you have a moment? *(To tiptoe (around) them—an imagery action) (To pacify) (To greet)*

Hot Person: Not now, I'm busy.

You: I think you really need to listen. *(To persuade) (To beg) (To negotiate)*

Remember, the Hot Person automatically modifies how the actions are executed. Persuading an intimidating person has a different flavor than someone who regards you as alpha, which is why you always, always use the appropriate Hot Person in a scene.

(By the way, if you're one of the rare people who isn't intimidated by anyone, try doing the mini-scene above and commit 100 percent to the suggested actions. Add the Body Language tips from that chapter in Part Three. You may not only create a believable performance, but you may also discover an emotional connection by working this way.)

In your Personal Scene, you used actions without being consciously aware. For example, in the Personal Scene chapter, Debra the real estate agent used the following actions in confronting her former client, her goal being to get him to admit he wronged her.

- She confronted him
- She accused him
- She unleashed (on) him
- She attacked him
- She demanded (of) him
- She guilted him

Debra didn't plan those actions; they happened organically because of her emotional connection. But if she were to recreate that scene, even after the circumstances of the Personal Scene lost some of its original heat, she could *identify* and *commit* to the actions as they originally occurred, which would in turn recreate the spontaneity of the original scene.

One of the reasons why I find the connection exercises like the Hot Person Confrontation invaluable is you can discover unique actions that you might not ordinarily choose working on a scene, and then employ similar actions working on scripted material. Look at the following speech. You can gather it's a confrontation.

"You think you're so hot, don't you? You're a nothing, a nobody. You never made it in your life, so you think you can get away with bullying and taking out your mediocrity on everyone else. You're a loser, and I've got news for you—you'll never get anywhere. I'm

going places, pal, and when I look in the rearview mirror, I hope I see your bloated, red, lowlife face for the last time."

An inexperienced student might make standard confrontational action choices. Yet this is a facsimile of the Hot Person Confrontation when Marvin had the fantasy encounter with his former football coach—the goal being to get his power back by speaking his mind. He found all of these other delicious choices organically, never once raising his voice. It was a brilliant scene.

- He mocked him
- He entertained him
- He mimicked him
- He chided him
- He dismissed him
- He parodied him

The advantage of being in class is you're exposed to so many other human beings and their natural reactions, which can inspire the choices you make and the potential actions you can choose. The actor who makes the unique action choice in a moment is quite often the actor who makes a memorable impression.

I mentioned earlier that I prefer to establish a connection to a scene first and layer in actions later. However, sometimes I do start with the Actioning method if I'm working on a gritty, violent scene that demands an emotionally heightened performance. I've found that choosing impactful actions for my dialogue not only creates rawness and spontaneity, it also takes the pressure off trying to imagine the circumstances of an otherwise grisly scenario.

For the movie *The Shadow Effect*, the second half of the audition was what I call the "Screaming Woman in Distress," where my character, Julia, walks into a scenario where her husband is being attacked on their vacation yacht. There were just three lines in this sequence, in the midst of the action where her husband is fighting off the attacker. Here is a facsimile of my audition dialogue.

(She emerges on deck and discovers the fight) "Oh no! Jack!"

(She runs in the boat and reemerges with a gun, hysterical) "Leave now or I'll blow your head off!"

(And as a last resort) "Get away from him!"

My objective was clear—*trying to save* my husband from the assailant, and in that light, I chose specific actions *directed toward the assailant* to make the scene more dynamic.

"Oh no! Jack!" *("To shock" the assailant. I chose "to shock" as an attention-getter, to throw the assailant off.)*

"Leave now or I'll blow your head off!" *("To threaten" the assailant.)*

"Get away from him!" *("To scorch" the assailant. This was a figurative image I used to literally scorch him with my words.)*

Committing to those actions gave me all the emotional fuel I needed to carry me through the scene. This was an audition I taped for casting and it resulted in booking the role.

If you're working on a set, coming prepared with an Action strategy helps you bring variety and more shades of nuance, especially if the director asks you to make another choice in a second, third, or tenth take. In the Hallmark movie *True Love Blooms* starring Sara Rue as Vicki George, I was lucky enough to be cast as Audrey, Vicki's mother. I had a natural affinity for Sara, so it wasn't difficult for me to feel motherly toward her, therefore Hot Person was automatically taken care of. (That's always nice!)

> And yes, when you have an affinity or a strong emotional reaction to the human being you're playing opposite, use it. Look into their eyes, let them affect you, and respond to them in the moment. That's the dream scenario we all hope for!

Audrey is sprinkled throughout the movie in short scenes that reveal who she is. In reading the script, I picked up clues that she is a strong, independent woman. She lost her husband at a relatively young age, so there is sadness there, yet she does not wallow in it and still manages to find contentment in her life, especially with her daughter. She wants Vicki to find her own strength, and offers motherly advice sparingly.

In our first scene, Vicki is in Audrey's home at dinnertime, airing her troubles about potentially losing her beloved community garden, started by Vicki's father and Audrey's late husband, to a developer. It's clear that Audrey's role is to be Vicki's sounding board, and inspire her to find a solution. When you watch the movie—see if you can identify the actions "to cheer," "to make her smile," "to reassure," "to (figuratively) tiptoe," "to intrigue," and "to steel."

How did I arrive at these choices? Most of these actions emerged organically at the audition by using Hot Person and a motherly Mode of Being (Part Three). After I was cast, I determined that Audrey's I Need was to support Vicki in becoming a strong, independent woman, and the actions I rehearsed with fell under that umbrella of care and comfort. However, I always come to set prepared with second, third, and even more choices if the director wants to see something else. I identified my audition actions and came up with some alternate possibilities.

Another helpful resource to find effective Actions is a book called *ACTIONS: The Actor's Thesaurus* by Marina Calderone and Maggie Lloyd-Williams, a British theatre director and actor respectively. They have compiled a thesaurus of action verbs for actors that they feel are the most effective for the method of "Actioning." If I am looking for inspiration for an interesting choice, I'll find a verb, like "to charm" and find all of the alternate possibilities: to allure, to amuse, to captivate, to enchant, to endear, to intrigue, to mesmerize, etc. During my rehearsal process I try the different choices, just like trying on dresses at the store. If one feels like a good fit and is the most truthful and effective in that moment, that's the one I pick.

The *ACTIONS* book also has a helpful section where they group verbs by category, like loving verbs or damaging verbs. Depending on the tone of the scene and your objective, you can go straight to those pages for inspiration.

The interesting aspect of this technique is our individual interpretation of a particular action verb. In the arbitration scene, my version of "to patronize" may be different from yours. My version of "to captivate" or "to torment" may be as well. So, by using this technique, you don't lose your individual stamp on your art.

Whether you choose to use Actions to enhance your scene work or follow the Actioning method to attack a script, I encourage you to try it both ways and make your own discoveries. After all, my Action choice for this book is to inspire you. I hope I achieved my objective.

ACTIONS EXERCISE #1 — ONE-WORD ACTIONS

When I first explain the concept of Actions to a class, I demonstrate the power of committing to an action by using one word, like "Hey," and choosing a strong action, like "to startle." I then direct my "Hey!" to an unsuspecting student in the front row. When they jump out of their seat, I've achieved my objective just by committing to that action.

You can experience the same power by working with at least one other actor and using one word, like "Hey," "Hi," "Oh," "Yes," or any other common word that we use in conversation. Taking turns with a partner, try each of them out with one or several of the following.

- To intimidate
- To thrill
- To flirt
- To intrigue
- To pester
- To warn
- To love
- To ignore
- To frighten
- To comfort

Notice the reaction you get from your partner with each action choice. Also take note if you were aware of an emotional connection as a result of committing to a particular action. As you discover more actions in your scene work, you can repeat this exercise as many times as you'd like with different actions of your choosing every time.

Actions exercise #2 — Changing Actions

This game will need a small group of people—two players, two callers, and an audience.

Make a list of action verbs, the ones that fit in well with the "I ... you" sentence, (e.g., "I attack you."). There are lots that fill the bill, like mock, flirt (with), taunt, annoy, seduce, hypnotize, charm, dominate, comfort, ignore, embarrass, etc. (Note that any action such as poke or torture is a figurative, not a physical action.) If you are using the *ACTION* book, you'll find lots of choices, but there are many other resources you can find online or just come up with your own verbs.

The two players will start the scene with audience suggestions like location and/or a relationship. Each player has a caller assigned to them that will freeze them in the course of the scene, calling their name and an action, which the player must commit to 100 percent.

Of course, in this game, the actions are random and don't follow true scene logic. However, it does illustrate how actions can be used and the freedom—and sometimes resulting emotional connection—the actors experience simply by committing to an action.

Actions exercise #3 — YOUR ACTION-OBJECTIVE SCENE

At the beginning of this chapter, I gave the example of drumming up students for my acting class. It was a situation where I needed to make something happen, but there was an obstacle in my way.

For this exercise, think of a time when you needed to make something happen, or to achieve a positive outcome in a situation, against the odds. It could be repairing a damaged relationship, competing for a difficult-to-get job, getting an airline representative to help you when you've missed a flight. There has to be an obstacle for you to overcome, which is the core of a dramatic situation. The obstacle could be your previous behavior (you drank during the relationship or otherwise hurt the other person), your resume (maybe you aren't as qualified as the other job applicants), or the qualities of the other human being (surly airline employee, intimidating boss, etc.). Choose your most difficult situation, even if it takes time for you to think about it.

Just like the Personal Scene, you will write this in script form. This time, however, you will identify the actions that you used in order to achieve your goal. If they don't come to you at first, start by writing the scene, then act it out, either by yourself or with a scene partner. Ask yourself, what am I doing in this moment or on this line?

Here's how I transcribed my scene:

ANDI
(knocking on a retail store owner's door)
Hi, can I come in? *(to make them smile)*

STORE OWNER
Yes, can I help you?

ANDI
I just moved to St. Petersburg and I'm trying to start an acting class ... *(to ingratiate)*

STORE OWNER
I sell art supplies — I'm not interested in acting.

ANDI
Oh, I know — I was just wondering if you could help me out. *(to befriend)* I have these fliers and I was hoping to post one in your window. *(to charm)*

STORE OWNER
Sorry, I have too many fliers as it is and I'm going to stop it. My window looks messy.

ANDI
Sure, I get it. *(to empathize)* You know, one of the reasons why I love it here is seeing the stores with fliers in

the windows. *(to connect)* It gives me a real sense of community. *(to warm)* It makes me love it here, so much more than Los Angeles. *(to touch her heart)*

STORE OWNER

Why did you move from Los Angeles?

ANDI

My husband and I needed a fresh start. *(to unburden)* Now all I want to do is teach. *(to share my passion)* I would so appreciate it if you gave me a break. *(to appeal)*

STORE OWNER

Well, okay, go ahead. And good luck with your classes.

Notice that all of my actions support sharing my love of teaching, my need for my classes to happen, and being vulnerable enough to ask for help. None of the actions demand, intimidate, harass, or are otherwise unpleasant. But if in your scene you are extracting an apology from a bully who bothered either you or a loved one, your actions would definitely take a different tone.

Actions Exercise #4 — Hot Person Intervention — The Sequel

If you did the Hot Person Intervention exercise in the I Need chapter, now with more detailed information about Actions, you can revisit the exercise from the Action perspective. Go back to your improvised intervention dialogue and note the actions that you used spontaneously to achieve your objective. Did you demand, confront, humiliate? Or did you convince, motivate, enlighten? The actions you chose would fall in line with your Hot Person's issues and your relationship with them—if they needed tough love, your actions would have been tougher. If they needed a gentler nudge, they would be more nurturing.

Quickly transcribe your improvised dialogue, and choose the most impactful action for each phrase. Now, either alone or with a scene partner who has a synopsis of the situation, with your written dialogue as a loose guide, do the scene again. As a reminder, your objective (I Need) is to persuade them to change their behavior and turn their life around. I highly recommend you record this scene.

See if this has the same power as your improvised version. If you felt your actions weren't clear or didn't achieve your objective, ask yourself if you were fully committed to achieving your objective or if you could have chosen different actions. This may or may not work for you, but identifying strong actions is still a valuable tool for you to have in your back pocket in case you ever need it.

ACTIONS EXERCISE #5 — ONE-WORD DIALOGUE SCENE

This is an exercise that is practiced in many acting classes and is a powerful way to get in touch with Actions, I Need, and the potential emotional connections that result.

Two actors are given a high-stakes scenario. Some that we've done in class are: nurse and dying patient, one person on the brink of suicide, two people in a car crash, two siblings fighting over an inheritance, a spouse meeting their partner's secret lover. For the dialogue, each actor may only speak a one-word sentence to convey an action, thought, or response. For example, in the suicide scenario:

ACTOR 1
Why?

ACTOR 2
Sad.

ACTOR 1
Help ...?

ACTOR 2
No.

ACTOR 1
Love!

ACTOR 2
Lonely.

ACTOR 1
Please!

ACTOR 2
Can't.

And so on. Because the dialogue is so minimal, the actors get quickly connected to their I Need, their Actions are clearly defined, and some have a very strong emotional response as a result. The actors in the above scene became very emotionally connected, as did the rest of the class.

PRIVATE MOMENT

That's what acting is—it's about ... having the courage to allow your audience into the private moments of your characters' lives.
—Kerry Washington

In film and television, not every scene has a Big Speech/I Believe moment, confrontation, or crisis. Intensity ebbs and flows in a feature film or a nighttime drama. There are quieter, private moments—especially if you're a lead character. Some scenes require no more from you than to just participate in the most mundane activities. In other words, act like a human being.

Now that you're doing your homework and watching an abundance of TV and film, you may have noticed these Private Moments, where the character is driving a car, working at a desk, reading a book, or just alone with their thoughts. The character is completely absorbed in their quiet activity, and in turn, we feel like voyeurs peeping through a window into their life.

For a great Private Moment, I'll never forget the scene in the movie *Unfaithful* when Diane Lane is riding the train from Manhattan back to her suburban home. She's just had a tryst with her lover and is mentally reliving the event that just occurred. While she's engrossed in thought, we see every kiss, touch, ecstatic moment replayed on her face. It's truthful and never pushed out or performed for us, rather the camera catches her very private moment that she's experiencing in a public place. In my opinion, that's the scene that earned her the Academy Award® nomination for Best Actress that year.

These Private Moments are the connective tissue that hold the big dramatic pieces of a movie together. When the actor is behaving as one would in real life, it draws us in and makes us feel like we're watching a real event. It makes the explosion or alien invasion in the following scene even more powerful.

Knowing when Private Moments can occur is also a key audition tool. At the start of a scene, quite often a character can be lost in thought or engrossed in an activity before they're interrupted by another character. This is quite often referred to as the Moment Before. Or they can ponder what just took place at the end of the scene after the other characters leave, which I call the Final Moment where the action continues even after the last line of dialogue is spoken. If you know how to incorporate these believable beginning and ending moments in your auditions and scene work, it can be the difference between a booking and the unemployment line.

When one of my students complained that they were having trouble relaxing on camera, I devised the following exercises to develop the muscle memory of natural, unforced behavior, using the camera as a silent ally. These are not performance exercises; they are behavior exercises. When you practice them on a regular basis, ideally, you'll forget the camera is even there.

PRIVATE MOMENT EXERCISE #1

When you have uninterrupted time, either at home or at work, turn on a video-recording device and set it up to have a clear view of you. Start an activity—painting your toenails, doing computer work, reading, making dinner. (When we do this exercise in class, I prefer these simple activities to scrolling through a cell phone. I want my students to be absorbed and thoughtful, not zoned out.)

Do the activity and make some observations. Are you noticing the urge to perform or be "interesting"? If you are, refocus on the activity or find an activity that requires more attention, like adding sums of numbers, composing a letter, or playing solitaire. This may take practice in concentration. My actors are instructed (and quizzed after) to not just scan a magazine, but to read the page. If you're writing notes, to not just scribble, but to write real sentences and thoughts. The more specific you are and the more purpose you give your task, the more focused you will be.

When you're finished (I suggest at least two minutes or longer), watch the video. You may notice the moment when you stop performing and are simply doing the activity. The "doing" is much more real and fascinating every time.

PRIVATE MOMENT EXERCISE #2

When you are relaxed on your bed or on your couch, set your video-recording device focused on your face. Recall your Hot Person Confrontation, either the one you've already done in the exercise or any other. Replay the confrontation in your head, not out loud. See the other person's face and feel your response to them. *Do not perform this for the camera—just experience it.* You've replayed these confrontations in your head before; now the camera just happens to be a witness. When you're finished, watch the video, and again take note—are you observing yourself experiencing a Private Moment or performing for the camera? If you caught yourself performing, do it again, focusing on the event. This may take some practice, and you may have to do it several times. After a while, you will become accustomed to the camera as witness to your truthful activity, and you will feel less inclined to perform for it. This is essential for your future on-camera acting work.

PASSIONATE ACTOR TAKEAWAYS

- Do the I Need exercise as a pathway to connect viscerally to your character's objective and desperate need. Remember, they will likely not be the same; however, getting in touch with your *need* gives you empathy for your character's need.
- Use the character's Mantra as a tool that can inform your behavior, drive the pace of a scene, and provide subtext.
- If your character has moments of strong convictions, opinions, or is on a mission to foster change, use the I Believe exercise to fill up your tank and connect from your core.
- Identify the Memory moments in the scene and plug in your own appropriate Memory moments, either from your own life or your imagination.
- Always note the Place where the scene occurs and explore how it impacts your emotional life and behavior.
- Use the Action technique to bring more definition to a moment or to quickly connect to a highly charged scenario.
- Note if there are any Private Moments in the scene, usually when your character is caught up in their own thoughts or an activity. An audition or a scene can begin with the character in a private moment before another character speaks (Moment Before), or end with a private moment at the end of the action (Final Moment)—look for those opportunities and practice, practice, practice to make it look natural!

PART THREE

THE PRAGMATIC ACTOR

The art of acting is not to act. Once you show them more—what you show them, in fact, is bad acting.
—Anthony Hopkins

MODE OF BEING

I imagined what it would be like to be a wizard. And then I pretended and acted in that way.
—Sir Ian McKellen, *Extras*

You just checked your email, and in the inbox is the coveted audition request, either from your agent or from your own self-submission. (There are many websites that post jobs for actors without representation.) The request usually has a lot of info—the names of producers, casting director, director, shoot dates, and hopefully the tone of the project. The character description may look something like:

"**BLAIR**, 25–40, any ethnicity, an upscale party guest. Two lines."

The script for the audition, otherwise known as the "sides," is attached. You see the circumstances are you've just arrived at the party, and you're being greeted by the host.

```
INT. UPSCALE MODERN HOME - NIGHT

                    BLAIR
                 (entering)
            Thanks for inviting me.

                    HOST
        Thank you for coming! We're serving
            cocktails in the library.

                    BLAIR
         Sounds fabulous! (exits to the
                  library)
```

You were given a key bit of information in your character description: upscale party guest. Have you been to an upscale party? If so, great. If not, have you met someone you would consider upscale, the type that wears Chanel and carries Louis Vuitton bags? (Not the knockoffs, the real deal.) Then you have most of the information you need to deliver a winning audition.

Up to this point, we've worked with your personal life as the raw material for your acting work. In lead roles and many other pivotal characters, I believe that is the best foundation you can use to connect to a script. But there are many roles that don't require deep personal exploration or emotional connection, but rather what I refer to as a Mode of Being.

A Mode of Being is an easily recognized archetype that we're universally familiar with. It can be a profession or personality type—like a doctor or class clown. It can have other identifying factors like age, economic status, nationality, regional accent, and/or attitude (e.g., Brooklyn). Or it can be a fantasy figure, like a space alien or a wizard.

These archetypes have a practical application in storytelling, especially on television. The plots move quickly, and we have just seconds to identify who a character is. We see a human wearing a white coat in a hospital, and we recognize a doctor. We see a burly human with a leather vest and tattoo on a Harley, and we know that's a biker. We see a woman with coiffed hair and pearls eating lunch on the Upper East Side in Manhattan, and we assume she's a socialite. These visuals are supported by the actor in the Mode of Being of these characters, behaving as we would expect in the given situation.

The Mode of Being approach is a quick way to connect to a character and their behavior, using your own experience, observation, or imagination. The Mode of Being can be expressed with any combination of body language, vocal tone, accent, sitting or standing posture, personality traits, activity (or lack thereof), affectations, attitude, and even wardrobe. Because of these physical factors, you as an actor are *using your body to tell the story of your character*. It's about your behavior and *committing* to the Mode. This can be called an *external* rather than *internal* approach to an acting role. But even with an external approach, you can still experience a personal connection.

Part of your job as an actor is to assess the type of role you're reading for and the tone of the project. You will get this information from the character description, along with the script that you'll be reading. As I previously mentioned, for big film and TV projects, you will usually only be given the sides with your character's lines.

The character description may read "Harry, 50's, used-car salesman" or "Ginny, 30's, flirtatious" or "John, 20's, party animal" or "Elaine, 60's, upscale" or "Reverend

Winston, 40–70, minister for Abby and David's wedding."

Given that none of these characters has a pivotal moment and are all smaller parts that move the story along, these are examples of the types of roles that you can connect to just by understanding their Modes of Being.

A used-car salesman is the perfect example of a Mode of Being character. When I say "used-car salesman," an image may pop into your head. We expect someone with an extroverted personality, someone who may have slick mannerisms and speech patterns from years of wheeling and dealing, who even dresses a certain way—maybe a checkered jacket and polyester pants.

A minister conducting a wedding is another perfect example of a Mode of Being character. We expect the minister to perform their duties in a warm and dignified manner, with a certain tone of voice and quality of behavior.

If the character description reads "flirtatious," that's the Mode of Being of a personality type or behavior. "Party animal" is a personality Mode of Being in a particular circumstance or setting. "Upscale" is the Mode of Being of economic status, which in turn affects a character's attitude and mannerisms. All of these modes inform how the character navigates a given situation.

And like Sir Ian's quote in Ricky Gervais's series *Extras*, a wizard or any other type of fantasy role is also a Mode of Being, created from our imagination or from our expectations from generations of fairy tales and folklore. McKellen is obviously being cheeky and making fun of the actor's tendency to overthink a role. And he's absolutely right. Sometimes all you need to do is pretend.

Mode of Being became an essential teaching tool after watching the "Annie's meltdown" bridal shower scene from *Bridesmaids* in class. In the scene, Helen tells Lillian her gift is a trip to Paris. The other guests erupt in applause, and then Annie famously throws the best tantrum in bridal shower history.

We had several women on stage for the scene—the three actresses playing the leads and many more as extras at the shower. However, the moment the scene began, it was an epic failure. A bridal shower is the ultimate chatty girly-girl event, but my actresses looked like they were getting colonoscopies.

We stopped the scene and discussed the Mode of Being at a bridal shower. If you're female, chances are you've been to one. It's happy! Oozing with girly talk and compliments! "I love your dress!" "How's Richard's new job?" "You look fabulous!" It has the frenetic energy of a henhouse on speed, fueled by champagne and estrogen. Voices are higher, louder, faces are smiley, laughs are forced but congenial, choruses of oohs and aahs erupt when presents are opened, especially the naughty ones.

After we identified the Mode of Being—upscale women at a bridal shower (economic status plus party circumstance)—we did the scene again with the actresses in Girly Shower Mode. It was like watching different human beings on stage. Their *behavior* was now organic—we felt we were watching a real bridal shower. Rather than coming off stiff and amateurish, they now looked like experienced performers. I asked them how they felt. The consensus was, happy, excited, like they had just been to a party. Aha! Personal connection! That was a nice lesson for the ladies—they got to experience how simply *committing* to that mode gave them freedom and a feeling of connection.

A bridal shower or any other kind of social situation is a good way to understand how we assume a new mode to fit the circumstances. We are in our party Mode of Being as soon as we walk through the host's door. The party situation almost always demands a more heightened version of you than you would have in your everyday life. It influences everything—your posture, your actions, your tone of voice, your body language.

Like the party Mode of Being, there are many others that arise from circumstances. You have a certain Mode of Being at your job. There is a particular Mode of Being at a church service, courtroom, hospital waiting room, football game, commuting on a subway, on a first date. There's also the mode you're in at home, with a spouse or pet, or reading this book—like the mode in the Everyday Scene and the Private Moment. *All of these impact your state of mind and your behavior in a given situation.*

You can also use Mode of Being to connect to a character unlike yourself. Many actors use this technique as a jumping-off place to attack certain roles. Johnny Depp often uses his powers of observation of other humans in his acting work, most famously using Keith Richards as his role model to play Captain Jack Sparrow in *Pirates of the Caribbean*. He used Richards's incoherent mumbling and other physical traits to create an Oscar®-nominated performance. It's not an *impression* of the other human, rather an *inspiration* that you can use as a starting point.

We also associate Modes of Being with certain professions, for example: pro wrestler, beauty queen, rock star, monk, Brooklyn truck driver, five-star chef, army chief of staff, surgeon, ranch hand, judge, game show host, mortician, CIA agent. You can observe nuances in their manner of speaking, posture, body language, confidence, humility, and power and incorporate them into your work. You may not audition to play a pro wrestler per se, but if a character description reads "Marvin, 40's, loses his temper in an over-the-top rant," you may find it helpful to use the wrestler Mode of Being to make great discoveries for your audition.

There are Modes of Being in personality types that you'll see demonstrated in an exercise later. These don't come from an official textbook; they're just a few that I've identified and have used in class and coaching sessions: Extrovert, Introvert, Narcissist, Life of the Party, Gossip Girl, High School Jock, Cheerleader, Nosy Neighbor, Braggart, Snob, Sexual Seducer, Know-It-All, Jokester, and my favorite, Asshole.

Are we talking about stereotypes? The negative definition of stereotype is clichéd, hackneyed, or an oversimplification. But we're talking about general universal similarities and observations. Have we observed that pro wrestlers are *usually* loud and flamboyant? Does a doctor *usually* have a professional demeanor? Are we *usually* respectful in church? When you interpret any of these roles through your filter, your point of view will come through and avoid any clichés. The Mode of Being can be used as a jumping-off point, a way to connect, to use your imagination, and when combined with your other tools, can empower you to craft a unique performance.

My student Dino was doing a scene from *Scream Queens.* He was playing the cocky character Chad and having trouble relating to the role. Dino tends to be shy and has confidence issues. We stopped the scene, and I asked him to think about the biggest, cockiest jock at his school. When he had the guy in mind, I had him assume his way of standing, of speaking, his overall body language and presence. We started the scene again with Dino embodying the Mode of Being of the Jock. Suddenly the scene clicked. Everything about Dino changed, even his diction. He strutted onto the stage, spoke with more confidence, and he got laughs with lines we couldn't even hear the first time. There was nothing cliché about it—he wasn't doing an impression of the Jock. It was still Dino, who had discovered a heightened version of himself. It was a great example of an actor snapping into a character using the observational Mode of Being.

If you tend to be introverted or have any other personality trait that you feel is blocking your acting work, Mode of Being is a way to step outside of yourself and take on someone else's characteristics. It gives you permission to behave in ways that you would never think to do in your personal life. It can help you quickly connect if you have limited time to prepare for an audition. I use this tool for coaching shy children—they may feel too inhibited to play the popular, chatty character, but when I ask them to embody the loudest kid at school, suddenly they're transformed. I've been able to turn around some auditions that at first seemed like a lost cause into competitive bids for a part.

Depending on your role, you can use the Mode of Being approach along with our previous exercises. Using your personal connection along with the Mode of Being can be an exciting way to make unique character discoveries. At the same time, I also have a few coaching clients who never, ever want to use a personal connection. One said, "The reason I became an actor is so I can be other people than myself." In those cases, we only approach a role using the Mode of Being. For large roles and small, we find the externals, character behavior and other attributes that make the character believable. The bottom line is—what works for you so that you in turn are the best casting choice for that film or TV project.

Imagine what it would be like to be a working film actor. And now pretend and act in that way.

MODE OF BEING EXERCISE #1

This is a fun exercise for class, but you can modify it and do it alone. It's a way to explore snapping into another persona and exploring their behavior. You can take note of discoveries you make and apply it to your future scene work and auditions.

The setting is a restaurant, with a table, chair, maybe some place settings. Actor #1 will be given a Mode of Being. Actor #2 is the Server. Actor #2's primary job is to serve Actor #1. The Server can have other props off stage—water, water glasses, plates, menus, etc.

Actor #1 enters the stage/restaurant in the given Mode of Being. The Actor's behavior starts upon entry, and as I instruct my students, even before entering the stage. The Mode of Being informs their body language and movement. For example, if one is assigned the Mode of Being of Introvert, they may timidly open the door, and shuffle into the room, barely making eye contact. When the Server greets them, they may mumble an answer and quickly take a seat, staring at the table.

> BIG NOTE: The Server also has a Mode of Being—Professional Waiter. The Server must not take over the scene and should not attempt witty dialogue to fill in the silences. In this exercise, silences are golden. They do only what is necessary in order to do their job—greet the Actor, bring a menu, take the order. Then they leave the stage and only reenter when necessary.

When Actor #1 is left alone on stage, they can make discoveries about their behavior. They might develop a tic or nervous habit, like tapping on the table or fiddling with the salt and pepper shakers. *Don't plan ahead of time what this behavior will be—allow yourself to discover it organically.*

If the Mode of Being is Life of the Party, they can chat and greet other "guests" in the restaurant. If they are Queen Bee, they may demand more attention from the Server. *Committing to the Mode of Being will drive your behavior.* I've seen firsthand when the actor fully commits, their mannerisms and dialogue flow effortlessly. The beauty of discovering behavior in this improvised mode is you can take your discoveries and apply them to your scripted work.

These are just some of the Modes of Being we've done in this exercise. You can discover some of your own: CEO, Cheerleader, Belle of the Ball, Kids' Party Clown, Ladies' Man, Motivational Speaker, 007, Used Car Salesman, Politician, Earth Mother, Most Awkward Person in the World, CPA, Super Fan, College Professor, Ex-Con, Aging Surfer Dude, High-End Escort, Midwestern Church Lady, Upper East Side Socialite, Appalachian Hillbilly, Teenage Model, Mobster, Codependent, Soap Opera Star, Psychic, Drag Queen, Former Child Star, Lottery Winner, Partyer, Hitman, IRS Auditor, Wallflower, Goth Girl, Class Clown, Buddhist Monk, Math

Genius, Annie Oakley, Marine Drill Instructor, Preppie, TV News Anchor, Wizard, Trailer Trash, High School Nerd. I want to emphasize—even though each of these Modes of Being conjure up certain behaviors and mannerisms, there is no right or wrong way of approaching any of them. The only requirement is to commit to the Mode 100 percent—that's what makes this exercise exciting and your results unique.

> BIG NOTE: If you are doing this alone, practice entering the room as various Modes of Being that I've listed or use your own. You can imagine the Server and other guests in the restaurant. Allow yourself time to "be with" this Mode for several minutes and see what comes up—your behavior, catch phrases, even how you laugh. You can do an "I Believe" in this mode. Notice if at any point you feel the same kind of connection as you have in previous exercises.

You can make discoveries in this exercise to file away for your future work. The slickness that an actor discovers portraying a Used Car Salesman, or the passion as a Motivational Speaker, or a silly laugh playing a Kids' Party Clown, may be a trait or "hook" that can be the key to connect to a scripted character, all because you worked on the external Mode of Being first.

Mode of Being exercise #2 — Asshole

This is one of my favorite exercises. It's simply an extension of the first exercise, but it deserves its own mention. Everyone gets to be an Asshole.

My definition of Asshole is someone who doesn't care what other people think. They have a freedom of movement that is uninhibited, a relaxation about them. They are completely uncensored and say whatever comes to mind. They're not necessarily malicious—they just do what they please, regardless of the consequences.

You've probably seen actors on talk shows assume the Asshole persona. They enter the stage, flop on the chair, sit with their legs splayed open. They spar and trade stories with the host, and if a story or joke bombs, they laugh as if it was the funniest thing they've ever said. Even if they're dying inside, the Asshole Mode of Being carries them through.

I give this exercise to my overly polite actors, because many times great acting demands the opposite of polite and nice—it demands pushing boundaries and going to uncomfortable places, to risk disapproval or being perceived negatively. Many lead characters—hero or villain, especially in action films and similar genres—take on the Asshole persona at one time or another, or throughout the entire script. It can be a very powerful Mode of Being. This gives my actor a taste of that power.

Actor #1 is the Asshole, and like before, Actor #2 is the Server. To be clear, being the Asshole is not necessarily about being mean or rude, although that can be a byproduct. It's about behaving without inhibition and not caring about the impact you're making.

The Asshole can enter the stage, throwing open the door. Before the Server has a chance to greet her, she can flop down on a chair and grab a menu. She can order something that's not on the menu and command the Server to get it. When the Server leaves, she can turn the music up on her iPhone and sing loudly to it. These are just suggestions of what can organically happen in Asshole Mode.

I'm not suggesting you become an asshole in your everyday life. However, the Asshole Mode is an example of using a Mode as a way to loosen up and use your power—not in one-note cliché-type performance—but in your body language, the way you sit, the way you behave, all in ways that aren't asking for approval. You'll discover a lot of freedom in that.

Enjoy!

MODE OF BEING EXERCISE #3— COMFORT ZONE CHALLENGE

In this exercise, the world is literally your stage. You get to embody a persona that is unlike yourself and take it out into the world.

I was in a play years ago where I was cast as a homeless junkie. As a chubby-cheeked former cheerleader, that was a challenge I relished. To test my character's believability, before rehearsal I walked the streets surrounding the theater in full Junkie Mode. My hair was disheveled, face dirty, clothes covered in grime. I walked unsteadily and mumbled to myself. Bystanders looked at me with pity and disgust. Some men offered me money for "companionship." (I guess the unshowered look was a turn-on.) As uncomfortable as I felt doing this, the experiment paid off, and the character became one of the favorite roles I've ever played.

Your challenge is to take on a personality type, accent, or any Modes of Being that we've previously discussed. Or come up with your own and try to choose one that's in opposition to who you are. Ask yourself, how do they dress, wear their hair? Do they have speech patterns or any particular mannerisms? If you tend to cover yourself up, try wearing something body conscious. Walk around a mall or visit an unfamiliar coffee shop. (Note: Please make sure you're in a safe, public environment.) If you're introverted, take on an extroverted personality and engage people in friendly conversation. If you usually dress casually, wear something upscale and take on the persona of someone with wealth and high status. Notice how it affects the way you move, talk, make eye contact. If you tend to be intimidated, put on a power outfit and address others with a commanding voice.

This is what is commonly known as a "stretching" exercise. You may make discoveries that you can use in future scene work, but more importantly, it's about getting you to take risks, to get you out of your comfort zone and to stretch your capabilities. Your reward may be a confidence boost in your own Mode of Being.

MODE OF BEING EXERCISE #4 — YOU

This is more of an observational exercise to become aware of your castability. When you start your acting career, you will quite often be cast for the very attributes that you present when you walk in a room. Whoever you are at this point in your life, own it and lean into it. Are you a surfer girl, a bookworm, a military type? Are you shy, funny, analytical? Do you talk with a lisp or have an interesting physical attribute? With the exception of a few famous actors who have the luxury of being able to transform their looks with prosthetics and wigs, your biggest asset is who you are and your unique physicality. If you have a trait that's different—even if you thought it was a liability—that may be your biggest selling point, or as I like to say, your Super Power.

Make a list of all the personality traits you naturally possess—both positive and negative ("I'm funny at parties" "I'm a jerk when I lose at poker") along with your special skills, hobbies, and work history. Now ask your friends, fellow acting students, and maybe a (nonthreatening) stranger or two how they perceive you. This will make you aware of your personal Mode of Being. The sooner you are aware of your key qualities that make you *you*, the better you will be at presenting yourself in casting situations and booking those coveted roles!

BODY LANGUAGE

I saw this character, this man, so clearly. I knew how he carried himself. Burdened. His shoulders were slumped like those of a much older man. I was imagining a man who carried himself a lot like my dad.
—Bryan Cranston, about his *Breaking Bad* character Walter White, in *A Life in Parts*

It's an unrealistic expectation to feel connected to every scene you do. If you're having an off day or are pressed for time or just aren't enthusiastic about the script, you may feel lost about how to approach a role. But in acting, as in life, there is always a workaround, and one of the most effective workarounds for an actor is use of Body Language.

I mentioned Body Language in the Mode of Being chapter, because Body Language is an important aspect of the Mode of Being. You experienced how your Mode of Being informed how you entered a room, how it affected your posture, how you sat in a chair. But it's important to single out Body Language as a separate tool and secret weapon that you can use. Body Language can tell the story of your character before you utter the first word. Using certain Body Language movement, postures, and even breathing techniques can even affect your character's emotional life—another way of working externally to reach the internal truth.

Quite often, beginning actors move around stiffly on stage because they're self-conscious—more worried about their lines and how their hair looks than behaving truthfully in the moment. But because you've now done exercises like the Personal Scene, Hot Person Mini-Scene, I Believe, I Need, and Mode of Being—your body now has an unselfconscious sense of ease and comfort. You've experienced freedom without any sense of manipulation or choreography, where *your body works in tandem with your emotional life to tell the story of your character.*

With these exercises in your back pocket, you can now identify and recreate the Body Language you discovered spontaneously when you were behaving naturally and emotionally connected to the moment.

Think back on the Hot Person Mini-Scene exercise. If you incorporated an entrance, what did your body naturally do when you confronted the person who makes you fearful? Did you stand erect, or were you slightly slumped over? Did you enter the room forcefully or more tentatively? You didn't preplan your posture or movements, but before you said the first word, your body told the story of your relationship.

Now think about the sexual chemistry Hot Person. There are as many possibilities of Body Language here as there are Hot Persons in the world, but let's assume your body showed more of a welcoming, inviting posture. Maybe you playfully tapped the ground with your foot, leaned into the person, even touched them. Again, your body tells a lot. Just go to any singles bar and observe the behavior. (Tell your significant other you're doing research.)

When beginning work on a scene, actors tend to focus solely on lines and memorization and disregard all of the physical possibilities of behavior and Body Language. If you're auditioning in person, the casting director makes up their mind about you within a few seconds. You can add so much to your auditions and your scene work by remembering the power of Body Language at all times, but especially at the top of a scene.

A good example of how a bad entrance can ruin a scene happened in class. In the *Better Call Saul* scene when underling attorney Kim Wexler enters her boss Howard Hamlin's office to advocate for Jimmy McGill (aka Saul), my student Jenny confidently strode into the room, plopped herself down on a chair, slapped one leg over the other and waved her foot back and forth. That happened to be a great Asshole Mode of Being posture but not appropriate for someone of lower status entering her boss's office to make a very difficult request. And because *your Body Language also affects your inner life,* she was not connected at all to the potentially perilous nature of the situation.

When the scene was over, I pointed out the Asshole entrance, which also implied the absence of an intimidating Hot Person. Jenny admitted that she did not have a corresponding one in her life. No one intimidated her. And she was finding it difficult to imagine a What If: What if Hitler was sitting at the desk? "I'd make fun of his mustache." A snake? "I'd kill it." What If's are tough for some people, myself included, and you can't always rely upon them.

So, as a workaround, I simply had her change her entrance and her posture. I instructed her to enter very carefully, as if a wrong move would set off a bomb. Her shoulders were slightly hunched, and her stride was much more tentative. And then—her voice followed. It was shakier. I could see her natural confidence had dropped. We were on to something, and now we had a compelling scene.

This was a great example of using Body Language when you are having difficulty with every other kind of connection. You may not connect using a Hot Person, Place, or your I Need. Even though finding an appropriate Mode of Being might help, it may not be enough. But if you know how to use Body Language as a tool—it can save your performance.

Owen Teague, who I collaborated with early in his career for some winning auditions, is a wonderful actor who uses Body Language masterfully in his work. As Nolan Rayburn on *Bloodline*, upon his first encounter with the rest of the Rayburn family, he shows complete disregard for their opinion of him. He swoops into his uncle's home and throws open the refrigerator door as if he owns the place. We knew so much about his character just by how he entered the room. *He used his Body Language to tell the story of who he was.*

Body Language isn't just an empty technique—it can actually change the way you feel. Do this right now: hug yourself and curl into a standing semi-fetal position. Hunch your shoulders and stand there for several minutes. Or sit in a chair and slouch for a while. Notice your inner life. If you feel vaguely sad or insecure, your body position has actually changed your emotions.

Now let's go to the other end of the spectrum. A while back, I watched a life-changing TED Talk by social psychologist Amy Cuddy titled "Your body language may shape who you are." She lectured about "Power Posing"—how standing in certain body-confidence positions can raise feelings of power. Stand erect with both arms straight up in the air like an open V, and hold that pose. Try doing this for two minutes but go as long as you can. You will feel an internal shift—your mood and your confidence will be elevated.

When you modify the confidence pose and just stand erect, or sit in a chair with your body open, arms crossed behind your head, these are great tools to use when you play authoritative, powerful characters. Notice how when you assume their posture and mannerisms, your mood will follow. If you assume these poses before a stressful situation, like an audition, you will immediately feel more empowered.

You can tell a lot about a relationship by body language, and good actors understand that. You may be thrown onto a set and have to establish an instant relationship with the other actor, sometimes an intimate one. Our natural inhibitions may hamper our ability to invade the other person's space, get close to the other human being. Doing the Hot Person exercise helps you discover and identify your behavior in a relationship. If you can recreate the same body language, you will be able to make any interaction look believable.

In the movie *The Shadow Effect*, I had a playful, intimate exchange with my husband, played by Mark Ashforth. We had just met an hour earlier, and now we were in a scene as husband and wife, alone on our private yacht. The script called for me to banter with him and serve him beer. I was also fighting nerves—we were on a tight shooting schedule and were told we'd only get one or two takes for each scene. No pressure! I consciously used some Body Language tools to establish our relationship. I played with my hair, crossed over to him suggestively, and immediately my instincts took over—I sat in his lap, fed him beer, and kissed him playfully. This was all unscripted and my most natural performance in the movie.

You can use Body Language to give better definition to certain character and personality types, especially involving high and low status. If you're not clear what status is, it's defined on Dictionary.com as "the position of an individual in relation to another or others, especially in regard to social or professional standing." There's high status, like the queen of England, your boss, whoever's in power on *Game of Thrones*, and low status, like the queen's maid, you in your boss's office when she's chewing you out, and whoever cleans the chamber pots on *Game of Thrones*.

A person of high status will enter a room with great confidence—maybe tossing a hat or a coat to an underling. (Remember Meryl Streep's entrances as Miranda Priestly in *The Devil Wears Prada*?) They will sit confidently in their chair or throne and make direct eye contact if you deserve their attention, or none at all if you are particularly unworthy. Their voice has a sense of fullness, and they tend to speak with certainty. Or if they choose, they may exert their power by speaking quietly, making you lean in to hang on every word.

A person of low status is, by contrast, deferential. Their entrances deflect attention. (Think about the servants entering the upstairs area of *Downton Abbey*.) Their posture is more inverted. They try to take up less space in the room. Their manner of speaking is more hesitant—perhaps halting and stammering. They rarely make direct eye contact, and if they do, they'll break it often.

I've already mentioned *Game of Thrones*. Their talented cast used Body Language masterfully. Alfie Allen's Theon Greyjoy seemed to shrink in size when he did scenes with his father (Patrick Malahide). It told the entire story of a lifetime of a son's low status and intimidation by his father without even uttering a word. Daenerys Targaryen (played by Emilia Clark) was first seen as an immature princess—forced into marriage and cowed by her bullying brother—but evolved into a powerful force to be reckoned with. As the show progressed, her posture became more erect and her voice conveyed dynamic confidence, telling the story of her growth.

Bryan Cranston, who in my opinion is one of our finest living actors, is a master of using Body Language to tell the story of his characters. If you haven't already seen *Breaking Bad*, one of the greatest TV series of all time, watch his earlier scenes as a broken-down high school chemistry teacher, beaten up by bad breaks and a lifeless marriage. His shoulders are hunched, his eyes are downcast and unfocused, his voice uncertain. As he becomes "Heisenberg," he transforms into a formidable, confidently powerful figure who faces down drug dealers and killers. In the famous "Say my name" scene, you see him at the height of his transformation.

I want you to be able to use everything you've got—your inner life plus your body—to achieve a three-dimensional performance at all times, whether you're delivering one line or carrying a movie. Here are some exercises that you can practice to not only get comfortable using your body to tell a story but also to find a character and an inner life with a more physical approach.

Body Language exercise #1 — Personality Dance

This is a favorite in my studio. It's using your body to tell a story by dancing to music.

The class volunteers a list of all types of emotions or states of mind, like "happy," "distraught," "raging," "drunk," "forgetful," etc. These are written on pieces of paper and thrown into a hat. Each student draws two of these and must now "dance" what they have chosen. They can pick their own music, but the most successful ones are usually techno, hard rock, classical, or jazz.

In the dance, exaggeration is encouraged! This is about having fun and experiencing a sense of freedom and even silliness. Get out of your head, get creative, and let your body tell the story!

Because there are two chosen personality traits, the dance can shift wildly between the two, especially if they're disparate in nature. The actor could be bouncing back and forth between "hyperactive" and "serene." That gives the actor even more ammo to play with and is much more fun for the audience to watch.

After a few minutes of the dance, the class guesses the emotion or state of mind that they have seen. It's amazing how often they're correct—even with the more nuanced, difficult-to-guess choices.

You can modify this exercise by choosing only one emotion to dance, but we find it more fun and challenging to do two. And to make it even more challenging, a teacher, leader, or non-participant can write all the choices in a hat before class so there's no hints as to what they're about to select.

How does doing a silly dance help your acting? Not only does it give you a great benefit by loosening you up—both body and spirit—but you may make discoveries that you can use later to develop a character. The Body Language that you discover spontaneously while dancing "hyperactive," even greatly exaggerated, can be modified into a subtler physicality if you're playing a similar character in a dramatic scene.

Body Language exercise #2 — Character Dance

This is similar to the first exercise, but rather than picking from a hat, each student will think of someone in their life with a distinct personality. The more they exhibit their personality through physicality, the better. For example, if they gesture with their hands wildly, or walk with a shuffle, or stand in an odd posture, or clean house obsessively. Emotional traits are incorporated as well—for example, if they have a tendency to explode, or mope in a corner, or laugh excessively.

The actor then chooses appropriate music and "dances" this character. They're encouraged to find their character's "hook"—whether it be a walk, a laugh, a weird gesture—and heighten it. If your chosen human has a bouncy walk and an outgoing personality, you can use those traits to create a joyful dance. In class, students have chosen a quirky spouse, a whimsical child, a ranting boss. One of our best Character Dances was the portrayal of a well-known local business owner known for screaming at underlings—done to heavy metal music!

How does this exercise help? The exaggerated dance trains you to let your body do the talking—to find a sense of freedom and above all non-judgment! If you are working on a role, you can use this as a warm-up to explore your character's mannerisms before you bring it down to a realistic level, now looser and freer in your character's skin.

Body Language exercise #3 — the Power Pose

Stand in the Amy Cuddy Power Pose that I described earlier: your arms up in the air, in a big V. You can stand still or walk around. Keep your arms up as long as possible, for at least two minutes, but try to keep them up until you feel an internal shift to a feeling of power.

Now, with your hands down but still in that groove, choose a monologue that requires a great deal of authority or high status. One of my favorites is Jules's (Samuel L. Jackson) speech in *Pulp Fiction*. Jules is the chief enforcer for his boss, Marcellus, and is now doing his bloody business of vengeance to square what was perceived as thievery, and an insult, to his boss. The speech builds to powerful climax, paraphrasing Ezekiel 25:17:

And I will strike down upon thee with great vengeance and furious anger those who attempt to poison and destroy my brothers. And you will know my name is the Lord ... [pulls out his gun and aims at Brett] ... when I lay my vengeance upon thee.

Riffing on the Quentin Tarantino inspiration, in the same Power mode, imagine that you're cast as a preacher delivering this verse from Psalm 27:1–3 to a packed church or any group that you are charged with inspiring:

The LORD is my light and my salvation—whom shall I fear? The LORD is the stronghold of my life— of whom shall I be afraid? When the wicked advance against me to devour me, it is my enemies and my foes who will stumble and fall. Though an army besiege me, my heart will not fear; though war break out against me, even then I will be confident.

BIG NOTE: If you want to feel the full impact of this exercise—try the text first without doing the Power Pose. Then, do the Power Pose and repeat the speech. Notice the difference?

Body Language exercise #4 — the inverted pose

Now try the polar opposite of the previous exercise. Sit in an inverted position. Hunch your shoulders, bend over, and hug yourself. Just sit there for several minutes. This position constricts your breathing, so you are not able to take deep, relaxing breaths. Feel how this affects you.

Now, in the same pose, try a monologue that requires deep sadness and a sense of powerlessness. There are many on the internet, but for a challenge, here is Gertrude's monologue from *Hamlet*, Act IV, Scene VII, where she tells Laertes about his sister's drowning. (Remember to begin practicing with American English before you switch to the Shakespeare-written text):

GERTRUDE
One woe doth tread upon another's heel,
So fast they follow. Your sister's drown'd, Laertes.

(LAERTES: Drown'd! O, where?)

GERTRUDE
There is a willow grows aslant a brook,
That shows his hoar leaves in the glassy stream.
There with fantastic garlands did she come
Of crowflowers, nettles, daisies, and long purples,
That liberal shepherds give a grosser name,
But our cold maids do dead men's fingers call them.
There on the pendant boughs her coronet weeds
Clamb'ring to hang, an envious sliver broke,
When down her weedy trophies and herself

Fell in the weeping brook. Her clothes spread wide
And, mermaid-like, awhile they bore her up;
Which time she chaunted snatches of old tunes,
As one incapable of her own distress,
Or like a creature native and indued
Unto that element; but long it could not be
Till that her garments, heavy with their drink,
Pull'd the poor wretch from her melodious lay
To muddy death.

Of course, you can use any of the concepts in the previous chapters in this monologue. You can use a Personal Scene, a Memory of a loss, or use your imagination: a What If scenario witnessing a beloved Hot Person's lifeless body. But if you are having difficulty connecting to a scene like this, or if you have to deliver an audition with a quick turnaround, try this pose before tackling your material. This body position will help guide you to an honest emotional place where you can begin your work.

Body Language exercise #5 — status

As I described earlier, there are distinct differences between high status and low status characters. This exercise gives you a chance to embody the physicality of both.

Using the following script, partner with another actor and choose your role/status. Notice the script is written nonsensically, which is the point. Your job is to use the script to *commit* to the status you're playing.

If you're High Status, allow yourself to strut around confidently. Or sit in a power pose with your legs on a desk. Use physical cues to get the Low Status actor to do your bidding. Maybe if you have no desk to put your legs on, use hand signals to command your Low Status person to become the human ottoman upon which you rest your legs.

Conversely, if you're Low Status, you are doing everything possible to please and defer to High Status. Maybe you rush to dust off the chair before they sit. Or hit yourself on the head when you look them directly in the eye or a similar error to show your self-disgust.

Be creative, think outside the box, and *don't just rely on the words in the script.* This script is your playground to act as outrageously as possible. You have permission to continue the scene and see where committing to your status takes you.

HIGH/LOW STATUS SCRIPT

Keep in mind how your mode drives your behavior and the action throughout. If you are the "Low," you are constantly seeking High's favor.

If you are the "High," you have many possibilities for activity. Are you reading a book? Arranging flowers? Going through your dandelion collection?

INT. HIGH'S HOME - DAY

(Note: We are referring to a book on a top shelf. If there isn't a real one in your acting arena, use the "space" version.)

LOW

I just finished your windows, is there anything else you need?

HIGH

I need to get a book from that top shelf.

LOW

But sir (ma'am) there's no ladder.

HIGH

I know. That's why I can't get the book myself.

(LOW does everything possible to get the book. Jumps, flails, climbs on chairs and finally retrieves the book.)

LOW

Here you go, sir (ma'am).

HIGH

It's the wrong book!

LOW

I'm so foolish.

HIGH

That's an understatement.

LOW

I am the worst possible servant.
I deserve to crawl on my belly.

HIGH

Then do it. What's stopping you?

(LOW starts to crawl. The scene can continue with improvised lines.)

Now, in the sense of fairness, reverse the roles. It's important you experience both.

The point is to exaggerate the high and low status, and to let your body experience them. When you do a more subtle dramatic scene, even though you won't be as demonstrative, you'll retain the muscle memory of your high and low status self.

Body Language exercise #6 — breathing/the Raggedy Breath

The theme of this chapter has been using your body as a vehicle to, well, *embody* the human being you're portraying. An easy tool happens to be one of my favorite coaching tricks—using your breath to connect to your character's emotional state. This is especially true in moments of fear and high tension. Watch a horror film or any of the *Walking Dead* franchise shows and notice how the characters are practically panting when they're under stress or attack. That's what I call the

"Raggedy Breath."

Start by inhaling and exhaling as if you've just run several blocks or walked up a flight of stairs. Or go ahead, get your cardio now by jogging in place for a minute. (Do just enough to increase your breathing rate, but do not hyperventilate or get to the point where you're feeling dizzy. If you are not in good physical condition, skip this exercise.)

Keeping the Raggedy Breath going, now say the words of this sample dialogue, using the Action *to alarm* your group in order to save them:

They're coming to get us. They're right outside the door.
Everyone has to leave—NOW!

I made those lines up but it's a typical example of a moment in almost any horror/sci-fi/apocalyptic movie or TV show.

Conversely, if your character embodies calm, you can use your breath to connect to their serene state. Take in a deep breath, hold it gently for a few seconds, exhale slowly. Notice how that naturally calms you down. Imagine you're a doctor in a scene comforting a patient and say this line:

It's all right, Mrs. Jenkins.
Everything is going to be just fine.

Use this breathing technique when playing any character in the Professional Mode of Being in the next chapter, and notice how it helps ground your feelings of expertise and quiet authority.

BODY LANGUAGE EXERCISE #7— BODY LANGUAGE SCENARIOS

This is a crossover exercise that incorporates Place from Part Two and lets you experience how your body language is affected by a particular place and the given circumstance. With a group of other actors, choose from the following scenarios or create your own. Depending on the scenario, you can do it with one or more actors on stage. These scenarios are very effective without words; however, if you choose, you can improvise dialogue.

Start by establishing your movement or posture according to the scenario. Do not rush this—allow your body posture to affect your inner life; let that land in your gut and drive your behavior. If you choose to add dialogue, wait for several seconds before the first word is spoken.

- First time in jail or holding tank, surrounded by more seasoned convicts
- In a doctor's office, waiting for results on a potentially grim diagnosis
- Waiting at a restaurant for a blind date
- In a hospital waiting room, waiting for the baby to arrive
- In the lobby waiting for an important job interview
- Entering a room to confront someone who has threatened or harmed a loved one
- In a Cabinet meeting with the president after a recent attack
- At a funeral home waiting to view a distant relative or acquaintance (not a primary relationship)
- The first few private moments at home after a spectacular date or romantic encounter
- Preparing to enter a room to confront a cheating partner
- At a bar in full seduction mode

Notice how committing to the scenario impacts not only your body language but your inner life. When you start to work on scenes, use this tool and experience for yourself how starting with your physicality brings truthfulness to your work.

DO YOUR JOB!

Sometimes you can have the smallest role in the smallest production and still have a big impact.
—Neil Patrick Harris

We've already discussed the concept of Mode of Being and how it can be applied to many different types of roles that don't require an emotional connection. One Mode of Being is so common in TV and film that it merits its own chapter: the Professional Mode of Being. Or as I say to my students—just do your job!

TV is loaded with what are known as procedural dramas. These are the types of shows like the *Law & Order* original series and spinoffs, the *CSIs*, *Criminal Minds*, and all others that involve attorneys, police officers, detectives, coroners, crime-lab technicians, expert witnesses, and other types of jobs associated with the genre. We are following the solving of a crime, the prosecuting of a case, or a judicial procedure. The professional's *main goal is to get the job done*.

There are also many other movies and TV shows that are not necessarily a procedural drama but have many procedural-type scenes in them. These dramas can contain scenes and subplots in places like a hospital, a doctor's office, or a political arena. And in other episodic shows like *Homeland, House of Cards, This Is Us*, there are dozens of other job-centric supporting roles: office workers, executive assistants, bartenders, receptionists, researchers, tech support, bank tellers, maître d's, nurses, to name a few. These are usually the costar type roles that move the story along.

I've coached actors for these types of roles in hundreds of auditions and counting. In movie and TV scripts, these professions have a distinct Mode of Being—an attitude, behavior, sometimes even their own lexicon—that we generally have come to expect from our real-life experiences.

We expect a judge to behave with a certain amount of decorum in a courtroom, a mortician to exude empathy in the funeral parlor, a college professor to assume an air of scholarly authority in a lecture hall. We expect a doctor to say a sentence like "Patient is hyperoxygenated with bag mask valve ventilatory support" as easily as we might say "Pass the clam dip." Certain professions have an intrinsic expectation of behavior and demeanor. If you can embody those authentically, you have a great shot at getting cast in one of these roles.

BIG NOTE: Professional behavior does not necessarily equal courtesy. Think of a server at a greasy spoon, a bored barista, a nightclub bouncer. They might be dismissive, uninterested, or plain uncivil. Some might not even bother making eye contact. Keep that in mind when you get those auditions!

As ordinary as these roles might seem to be, I think they have the potential to be extraordinary. There's a brilliant example of this at the end of the movie *Captain Phillips* starring Tom Hanks in the title role. Based on a true story, Captain Richard Phillips's ship, the *Maersk Alabama*, had been hijacked, and his crew was held hostage and abused by a gang of Somali pirates. After their rescue, Tom Hanks was being examined by a navy doctor who asked several routine questions about his health and state of mind. (This clip is currently on YouTube, titled "You're Safe Now.")

As great as Tom Hanks was in this scene—I was watching the doctor. She was so understated and authentic I felt as if I was a fly on the wall on that ship. It seemed more like documentary footage than a movie. Her manner, or Professional Mode of Being, was a textbook mixture of competence, professionalism, and just the right amount of empathy to get her job done. She exuded experience and the questions she was asking seemed part of a routine examination that she had performed hundreds of times before. It was a brilliant counterpoint to the post-traumatic stress of Hanks's character and was absolutely riveting. Who was that amazing actor?

I then found out they hired a real navy doctor, Danielle Albert. She was directed to improvise the scene based on her real-life experience and what she typically would do in that situation. Ahhh, if only an actor could pull that off as authentically.

This became a challenge that I brought into class. Every actor should strive to be that believable in the types of professional roles that they will likely read in their career. Every actor's goal should be for the audience to ask, "Wow, did they get a real _____ to play this?" That is the gold standard we should shoot for.

You may read for these types of roles anytime in your career. Nowadays, casting pushes for variety in professional roles—it's possible to be any age, ethnicity, gender, shape, or size to be considered a professional. The size of the role can range from one line to several pages. For many of you, it might be the first acting job you book.

As you've seen by now, all of the exercises in this book are about identifying a type of moment or connection that you will be using in your auditions and scene work. For the Professional Mode of Being, you will learn how to access your own experience and use the *confidence* and *familiarity* you already have to connect with a script. Even if your only skill is making a tuna sandwich, you can use it to play a doctor. At least on TV.

Do Your Job! Exercise #1 — Your Knowledge Base

Think about the job you currently do. Every actor does something besides acting. It can be professional or menial—it doesn't matter. If you don't have a job, think of a skill you have—something you do really well. I'll wait.

Now describe that job or task in minute detail, step by step, as if you're training another person to take over your job. Assume they have zero prior knowledge of this field, so don't use shorthand. For example, if you're a hostess in a restaurant:

I show up to work at 4 pm, hang my coat up in the back room, find my punch card in the metal file, and punch in to the clock. I check in with my manager and take notes of anything I need to know for that night. I write down the specials on the blackboard in the entrance. I go to my hostess station and wipe down the menus with a damp cloth. I toss the damaged menus in the wastebasket. I sort the menus—cocktails and wine list in one pile, dinner in another, desserts in another. I check the messages on our voicemail and adjust the reservation list, adding or erasing names. I call the reservations to confirm and make any changes necessary. When the customers show up, I'll take them to their tables and hand them their menus. If they're not happy with their table, I'll reseat them or bring them back to the front and offer them a drink while they're waiting. Sometimes, I'll have to rework the seating plan like a jigsaw puzzle. If we're busy, I'll help the waiters bring out the orders. At the end of the night, I clean my station and write down the reservations for the next night.

And so on.

After an actor does this in class, I'll ask them how they feel. I can't think of a time when they didn't say relaxed and confident. That's because you are operating from your Knowledge Base, which will from now on be part of your muscle memory whenever you need to exhibit a sense of quiet power and confidence. Your Knowledge Base is a perfect starting point to play any professional role.

Now, using that Knowledge Base, with the same kind of comfort, confidence, and familiarity that you recounted your own job, read the following scripts. These were written for me by experts in each field and contain the type of language, including acronyms, that could pop up in a script. Make sure you highlight any word that's unfamiliar and verify the pronunciation, saying it several times so that it rolls out of your mouth easily. Your intention is to instruct another person, to share your knowledge with them. Your Professional Mode of Being is calm, knowledgeable, and expert. You've been at this job for at least ten years. The most important thing is to stay connected to the *muscle memory* of your Knowledge Base.

> BIG NOTE: In order to avoid the robotic trap, for #1 and #2, imagine you're speaking in confidence with a coworker who's also a very good friend. Make these two as much like your Everyday Scene as possible. For reference, watch any *CSI* episode.

#1 — (ER Doctor talking to colleagues) *Patient placed on cardiac monitor, ATLS protocols were followed.* (Points out the following areas on an X-ray.) *Patient had an obvious open fracture with a gunshot wound to the left elbow with marked angulation and disarticulation of the distal humerus to the proximal radius and ulna.*

#2 — (CEO talking to associate) *These financial projections are looking good, although you'll need to justify the static year-over-year expenses. Investors will know that the CAGR is unrealistic; contrasting to the industry average, you should anticipate about 12% conservatively.*

#3 — (Army sergeant talking to superior) *Sir, the LLRP's just got back from their recon and set up an LP 200 clicks to our nine. It gives them fire for 400 clicks up and down the LOC. The FO's are set to commence directing the CAT run at 1300 hours, and we are set to cross the LD at 1305.*

Notice how you felt. This type of language in the Professional Mode can throw many actors, especially in the beginning. But everyone in my studio who uses this Knowledge Base approach has a jump-start when dealing with this type of material. They tap into their own confidence and expertise, and it carries over into the script.

> BIG NOTE: When dealing with difficult words, here's a tip for what I call "American Mush Mouth." We are typically lazy speakers and tend to slur our pronunciation. When you're practicing these passages, speak very slowly and overenunciate every word. That's a good stretching exercise for your diction and will elevate your auditions to a more professional level. (My theory why British actors win meaty American roles? They talk real good!)

Do Your Job! Exercise #2 — Walking and Chewing Gum

In the hostess example in the previous exercise, the hostess had activities related to her job. When you did the exercise, chances are you also described the activities required for your job or skill. That's the thing about a job—you're usually doing something (or at least pretending to).

The other day, I was in the doctor's office, getting my blood drawn. I noticed how the nurse continued chatting while seamlessly prepping my arm, wiping the area with an alcohol pad, tying a tourniquet around my bicep, inserting the needle, and filling several tubes. (Note to self: remind people not to eat while reading this chapter.) Humans are constantly doing these Walking and Chewing Gum tasks in their daily lives.

In procedural dramas, many times you'll see a professional involved in an activity. A coroner examining a corpse, a crime lab technician peering into a microscope, a doctor studying an X-ray, a detective brushing for fingerprints, a mechanic working on a car while being interviewed by the cops. Chief O'Brien in *Captain*

Phillips was constantly active while she was interviewing Tom Hanks.

To play these types of professional characters, you need to get used to the concept of Walking and Chewing Gum. In other words, multitasking—something you do every day.

For the exercise, you will memorize the following dialogue excerpt:

(IT Worker to colleagues) *This server is overloaded: consistent 89% memory usage and 95% CPU activity. To combat overheating, we'll need to build a new spec, preferably with SSD and EEC, and initiate data mirror recovery. We will also need to reconfigure the redundancy architecture, perhaps a firewall constructed in the likeness of a centrifugal barrier. We have a limited amount of terabytes to complete this task for full encryption.*

Oh yes, it's heavy lifting—get used to it! Now using your Knowledge Base in Professional Mode, you will imagine a conversation with a colleague using those words while either: a) sorting a deck of cards into suits, b) sorting a pile of change into quarters, dimes, nickels, and pennies, or c) threading a needle and stitching a piece of fabric. The challenge is to *concentrate* on the *activity* while having the conversation.

In the beginning, many actors do a stop-and-start approach. They'll say a couple of words and stop speaking while they find a quarter. That's incorrect. The point is to walk *and* chew gum, meaning do both simultaneously. Since it's only three lines, you can continue the activity and repeat the lines as many times as you need until it starts to flow.

> BIG NOTE: If you're lucky enough to get cast in one of these roles, it goes without saying that the day before your shoot, you would rehearse these lines over and over, as many times as necessary until they're second nature. That's the way to prepare like a pro, and the director will love you for it!

The most successful, and most difficult, version to master is to be so involved in the activity that the words are of secondary importance. It's the kind of behavior we recognize as natural because we see human beings do it all the time. They have a split focus, but most of the focus is on the business at hand. If you've been in a long-term relationship, have you ever tried talking to your partner while they were fixing the plumbing or applying mascara? That's what I'm talking about.

These exercises are not only good for sharpening your memorization skills, they get you accustomed to being involved in an engrossing activity. It takes the onus off of *you* in your scene work—you no longer need to be self-conscious because you have to take care of business.

I think it's important to point out the similarity between these exercises in the Professional Mode and the Everyday Scene. A great majority of these types of characters and scenes are in this type of relaxed, everyday, competent mode while completing some sort of task. When this becomes second nature to you, your acting will be all the more natural and riveting to watch, and you will be on your way to playing the Professional Mode of Being like a pro.

Career Personality Types - I mentioned earlier that being a professional does not necessarily equal courtesy. By the same token, some jobs—or careers—may attract certain personality types by the very nature of their work. Most nurses I know genuinely care about other human beings and have nurturing personalities. Police officers and other law enforcement professionals might have been attracted to that career because of a need to catch the "bad guys" in order to protect the "good guys," maybe because of an event early in their lives. That can include comic book heroes—Batman decided to devote his life to catching criminals after witnessing the murder of his parents as a young boy. If you're a playing a professional, think about their potential origin story and the reasons why they chose this career. This may give you an even deeper level of connection to their humanity.

WATCH YOUR TONE! (the sequel)

Comedy's my first love. I love that so much. You play comedy in drama, too. The difference between genres doesn't really change the method of acting.
—Emma Stone

In our first episode of *Watch Your Tone!* (Part One), we saw our hero, Andi, thwarted in her attempt to impress a casting director with her comedic genius by the highly trained but tone-deaf actor Dick. The sequel opens some years later with Andi hunched over her laptop:

INT. ANDI'S OFFICE - NIGHT
The room is dark except for the laptop glow on Andi's face. She is typing furiously, muttering to herself.

ANDI
So, they think I'm obsessed, do they?
I'll show them obsessed.
I'll write a whole chapter about it.
No, wait, I'll start with a small chapter in one section… and then I'll write a BIGGER chapter in another section. And I'll *make* them read it.
Because as God is my witness…

(SMASH CUT to overhead crane shot of Andi with arms outstretched, à la Tim Robbins in *The Shawshank Redemption…*)

NO STUDENT OF MINE WILL EVER LOSE AN OPPORTUNITY BY NOT UNDERSTANDING TONE
… AGAIN!!!

Yes, that is my mission. You may not win every role you audition for, but I'll be damned if you don't book it because your audition didn't jibe with the project's tone. As I said in Part One, I strongly believe that recognizing different tones and having the flexibility to incorporate various tones into your performances is one of the most essential keys to becoming a working actor.

So, back to explaining tone as it relates to a film or TV show. It's not only the genre of a project—as in drama, romantic comedy, action adventure—but as I define it, tone goes into finer detail. It's the sum of the many parts that compose the mood and style of a project: how the dialogue is written, the pace of the dialogue and/or action, the setting and the types of characters on the show. The tone of a show is also portrayed visually with the color palette, set decor, and wardrobe, as well as how the actors are framed (close-up vs. wider shots), brightness or dimness of lighting, and resolution quality (sitcom "sharp" vs. courtroom drama "grainy").

All of these factors are clues that point to a show's tone and must be taken into consideration when you read for a role in that show. For an audition, smart actors modify their appearance and acting choices to emulate that tone, showing that they could seamlessly fit into the big picture that carries out the producer's vision.

To match the tone of *The Marvelous Mrs. Maisel*, you would have to effortlessly master the pace and wit of the dialogue, as well as styling your hair, makeup, and wardrobe to represent the early-sixties vibe. For any show in *The Walking Dead* universe, your character might be desperately confronting a life-or-death situation, dressed in the drab paramilitary style seen on that show. For a live-action (meaning human actors, not animation) Nickelodeon comedy, you would embody higher energy and playfulness, wearing brighter colors that shout "I'm fun!"

BIG NOTE: While we're on the subject of auditioning, remember I mentioned that tone is portrayed visually by how the actors are framed in a shot? When you start doing your copious research watching TV and film, notice that sitcoms use a lot of wide shots (where you see the actor's entire body) as opposed to close-ups used in drama (where their face and shoulders fill the entire frame). Why? Broadly speaking, an actor's physicality is featured in comedy, whereas an actor's thoughts and inner life are key to drama. Keep this in mind for your self-tape auditions!

Are you starting to get the picture? As you progress in your career, you will find researching a project's tone one of the most fun and challenging aspects of the audition process. The tone of both TV and movies is driven by current trends, the era they originated, and the creative forces both on and off-camera. I've categorized some commonly occurring television genres with broad descriptions indicating their accompanying tone. (Note that shows grouped in the same genre category might have a completely different tone, e.g., many on the Dramedy list.) Some of my observations are commonly held; some are my own opinions. I want you to start drawing your own conclusions to achieve world domination with your auditions, one tone at a time.

I believe that smart actors should understand entertainment from the past and how we've evolved into our present-day acting styles. Which is why I'm starting with...

Old-School Situation Comedies

In the early days of television, comedies followed more of a jokey formula—there was a punchline and canned laughter around every six seconds or so, and the style of acting was a little more exaggerated than what we're used to seeing currently. A classic example is the sitcom *I Love Lucy*. Lucille Ball was the star, playing a wacky housewife who was always getting herself into messes. She was also a master of physical comedy. *I Love Lucy* was the foremother of dozens of sitcoms to follow in the fifties, sixties, and seventies, like *The Honeymooners*, *Gomer Pyle USMC*, *The Dick Van Dyke Show*, *The Andy Griffith Show*, *Bewitched*, and many others. If you watch these shows, you'll notice a range of characters and acting styles from subtle (Andy Griffith) to over-the-top kooky (Paul Lynde as Uncle Arthur in *Bewitched*). Most of our modern sitcoms don't rely as much on the bigger acting style or the kooky characters, and yet these shows are still fun to watch, and it's valuable to know this style of comedic acting. A great example of how old becomes new again was on full display in *WandaVision*, where the first few episodes paid homage to older sitcoms.

Sitcoms of the Seventies and Eighties

In this era, some classic sitcoms emerged, for example, *The Mary Tyler Moore Show*, *The Bob Newhart Show*, *Cheers*, and *Taxi* to name a few. Titular stars Mary Tyler Moore and Bob Newhart were the "normal" people surrounded by a cast of oddball characters. *Cheers* and *Taxi* both featured clever writing and ensemble casts that played a more grounded, realistic level of comedy, even though *Taxi* featured the outrageously wacky Andy Kaufman and Carol Kane as Latka and Simka.

Sitcoms Starting from the Nineties

TV comedy began to transition to a more modern tone in the 1990s, starting with *Seinfeld* (technically it premiered in 1989), *Friends*, *Will and Grace*, and later *The Big Bang Theory* and *How I Met Your Mother*. In these shows, even the wackier characters are more grounded—like Phoebe on *Friends*, Karen on *Will and Grace*, and George on *Seinfeld*. I could devote an entire chapter to *Seinfeld*—I use it as an example in class about great actors being 100 percent committed to the situation, no matter how ridiculous. Remember Art Vandelay, the latex salesman? If not, go watch it now (*Seinfeld* "The Boyfriend," Season 3, Episode 17). It's a master class in comic acting.

Sketch Comedies

Another important comedic tone is, of course, sketch comedy, which my former scene partner, Dick, was completely unfamiliar with. The most classic example is *Saturday Night Live*, which for the past forty-plus years has been the most popular sketch comedy show on TV. On *SNL*, characters can range from larger than life, like Bobby Moynihan's Drunk Uncle, to a little more nuanced, like Cecily Strong's Girl You Wish You Hadn't Started a Conversation with at a Party.

SNL and many of the aforementioned sitcoms are/were performed live in front of a studio audience. They have more of an energy and heightened performance sense about them. There is a distinct difference between the tone of these comedies versus comedies that are called single camera, filmed on location without a live audience like *Key and Peele*, *Broad City*, *Inside Amy Schumer*, and *I Think You Should Leave with Tim Robinson*. (Of these, only *I Think You Should Leave with Tim Robinson* is currently in production as of this writing, but new sketch comedies are popping up all the time.) Key and Peele are known for inventive characters, and Amy Schumer generally plays herself in high-concept comedy sketches. These shows combine comedy with social parody, and even though the situations can be wacky, the actors play the situations in a more realistic, nuanced tone.

Kid/Teen Comedies

Remember how I started with the old-school situation comedies? The kid and teen sitcoms (on Disney, Nickelodeon, and other similar channels) are the modern-day version of that joke-based, broadly acted comedy style. The leads get entangled in zany situations, and the supporting characters tend to be archetypal versions of the Nerd, Spoiled Rich Girl, the Jock, the Bully, Smart Ass, Jokester, Ditz, Know-It-All, and Bratty Sibling. The tone isn't subtle—it's *big*—but that doesn't mean bad acting. You recall the term High Stakes (from Key Terms), meaning the urgency and importance of a situation. In a drama, that could be a meteor hurtling toward Earth. In a teen comedy, High Stakes could be a pimple on your forehead the night of the prom. Oh, the end of life as we know it! It takes a skillful actor to pull that off truthfully and get big laughs.

Present-Day Comedies

The new wave of TV comedy has more of a subtle tone compared to the old sitcom wacky/joke formula. One of the best and first of this era was *The Office*—starring Ricky Gervais in the British version and Steve Carell in the US. This show was filmed documentary style and followed the lives of the employees of the Dunder Mifflin Paper Factory, both in action and their "talking-head" interviews (where they speak straight to camera, among the many times the characters broke the fourth wall). The humor arose from character behavior: Steve Carell as the socially tone-deaf and cringeworthy Michael Scott, and Rainn Wilson's deranged Dwight Schrute led the cast of other quirky characters interacting with each other in their office setting. The tone of the show was deadpan or matter of fact—the antithesis of a joke-based comedy. Michael Scott would say and do outrageous and idiotic things, oblivious to the reactions of his fellow workers. The actors mastered the tone of believability and commitment—never commenting on what they were saying or doing. Other popular shows that followed suit are *Modern Family* and *Parks and Recreation*.

Modern comedies reflect a range of styles and are constantly redefining comedy's edges. Shows like *Catastrophe*, *Insecure*, and *Breeders* focus on the dark side of relationships in a conversational and dryly underplayed style. *Arrested Development* features great actors like Jason Bateman and Jeffrey Tambor playing absurd situations truthfully. The dark premises of *Unbreakable Kimmy Schmidt* and *Crazy Ex-Girlfriend* (kidnapping and stalking) result in optimistically goofy comedy and in the latter, clever music videos. *Jane the Virgin* mines the telenovela genre for laughs. *Maniac*, starring Emma Stone and Jonah Hill, pushes the definition of comedy by its setting in a pharmaceutical lab with surreal images of drug trials.

As comedies continue to become more sophisticated and explore new territory, they demand great actors—not just funny people. Even if you don't consider yourself comedically gifted, I encourage all of my students to do comedy scenes. If you can master comedy, you can do anything, or as the old punchline goes, "Dying's easy—comedy's hard!"

Episodic Television

Swinging over to the dramatic side of tone, you may have heard the term "episodic TV," which is the big-tent term for television drama, since most TV shows have storylines that unfold over many episodes. Even though comedies can also technically be episodic, usually when an actor says, "I booked an episodic," they're likely talking about an hourlong dramatic show.

In drama, there are even more subgenres than comedy. When you watch a variety of content, you will start to observe what makes them distinct: pace, dialogue, humor or lack thereof, acting styles ranging from realism to heightened, almost classical drama, even the color palette of each show.

Dramedies

Straddling the middle ground between comedy and drama is the dramedy—where there is a blend of dramatic and comedic themes. This category is *huge*—probably the largest and most popular genre on television. One of the most recently popular is the *Breaking Bad* spinoff *Better Call Saul* starring Bob Odenkirk. Also in the category are *The Marvelous Mrs. Maisel, Desperate Housewives* and its sister show *Devious Maids, Shameless, Monk, Gilmore Girls, Glee, Grace and Frankie, Nurse Jackie, Scrubs* ... just do an internet search of "dramedy" and you'll find hundreds of examples. Most of these shows will always be available to watch on streaming networks.

The heart of a dramedy can be a dramatic setting or situation, but it has comedic elements. *Devious Maids* is an episodic with a serious matter at its core—Marisol Suarez (Ana Ortiz) trying to exonerate her son charged with murder, but the other characters and situations tend to be lighter and quirkier. The title character Nurse Jackie, played by Edie Falco, is a drug-addicted nurse in a hospital, facing life-and-death situations with a sense of dark humor.

Some might be tempted to call *The Marvelous Mrs. Maisel* a comedy, yet there are dramatic elements in which the lead Muriel Maisel, played by Rachel Brosnahan, is divorced by her husband and begins a career in stand-up comedy. In *Better Call Saul*, while the supporting cast tends to play it straight—the more comedic elements arise from Bob Odenkirk's performance as a well-intentioned but misguided conman. His cons are funny, but as he fails to prove his worth to his mentally ill, judgmental brother, the circumstances turn tragic, and we watch him devolve into a shady criminal lawyer. This show really deserves to be in its own category but to keep things simple, I'm listing it here.

Procedural Dramas

Another big category on the dramatic side of tone are the procedural dramas featured in the Do Your Job! chapter. That would be any of the *Law & Order* franchise, all of the *CSIs*, and any other show with police, detectives, criminals, judges, witnesses, coffee, donuts, and a dramatic musical score. Unless you're the witness breaking down and confessing to the crime in the courtroom, the tone is generally professional and straightforward, and each episode is usually focused on the solving of a crime. The procedural drama is known for standalone episodes—usually one crime per episode that does not carry on to the following week.

Daytime Soap Operas

Also common in the dramatic department are daytime soap operas. I have always found it hard to relate to the campy plots and the sometimes-overwrought acting style, but it's still a genre you need to be familiar with. The characters tend to be stereotypes—the Ingenue Male and Female, the Bitch, the Hot Bad Boy, the Matriarch and Patriarch, the Good Doctor, the Evil Twin, etc. The situations have all kinds of outlandish and fantastical twists and turns—multiple marriages and divorces, affairs, amnesia, kidnappings, disease, comas, and miraculous recoveries. The characters are usually on the cusp of or in the middle of an extremely intense emotional situation bordering on the melodramatic. It's not an easy genre to pull off believably, as there are traps that can lead to overacting, but some of our finest actors, like Julianne Moore, got their training there.

Primetime Soap Operas

And then there are the nighttime, or primetime, soap operas, where the themes revolve around the good, bad, and ugly of family, business, and political relationships, enemies, lovers, jealousy, and power. There usually is a strong villain or villainess who drives the story and is a constant threat to the other characters. Although the plots can be soapy and the dialogue slightly affected, the acting style is more nuanced than the daytime soap. Some feature plotlines of teen characters, like *Outer Banks*, *Riverdale*, *The OC*, and *Gossip Girl*. Shows like *Dynasty* and *Dallas* originated more than a generation ago and had recent reboots. Also under this tent are *Nashville*, *Empire*, *Revenge*, and *Scandal*, to name a few. Kerry Washington's performance as Olivia Pope in *Scandal* is a great example of a talented actor elevating primetime soap material into riveting drama.

Family Dramas

Family dramas are also in the primetime soap category, with the focus on family relationships and a warmer vibe. Even if there's a conflict between family members in a family drama, it's usually resolved in loving ways we all wish our families could have embodied when we were growing up. Every generation seems to have an iconic family drama, going back to *The Waltons* in the seventies, *Little House on the Prairie* and *Thirtysomething* in the eighties, *Party of Five* and *Life Goes On* in the nineties, and more recently, *Dawson's Creek*, *Friday Night Lights*, and *Parenthood*. The hit series *This Is Us* seems to be the family drama of the current generation with a unique storytelling style that travels between the past and present in the life of the Pearson family.

Medical Dramas

Medical dramas are another subset of the primetime soaps—shows like *Chicago Med*, *Grey's Anatomy*, *ER*, *New Amsterdam*, and *The Resident*. A hospital or medical practice and sick people provide the backdrop for the relationships of the doctors, nurses, and the other medical personnel. Even though the relationships provide the soap element, the medical portions are infused with realism. If you're auditioning to be a doctor on one of these shows, it'll be expected for you to master the medical vernacular and portray the same gravitas as an experienced medical professional.

Legal Dramas

Legal dramas—see medical drama but insert *legal*. These shows are usually populated with the behind-the-scenes doings of attorneys, both in their law offices and in bed, and of course, dramatic courtroom scenes. The most recent popular shows include *How to Get Away with Murder, The Good Wife, Boston Legal, Suits, The Practice*, and *Damages*. The *Law & Order* franchise, mentioned above in the procedural category, had great courtroom scenes in the second half of almost every episode, so it also qualifies for the legal drama category. You could make the argument that any of these shows have procedural elements, however, they mostly emphasize the legal process, and the characters are better dressed.

The Golden Age of Television

There are many dramas that share in common a more realistic tone of writing and acting. You may hear descriptors like "gritty," "real-life," and other adjectives indicating these are shows that are going to take you on a ride that won't have the usual Hollywood happy ending. They usually have some combination of violence, strong language, and (more graphic than usual) sexual situations. Even though *Bloodline* was about a family, the tone was far from family drama. The situations were at times violent and tragic, and the acting style was so realistic that it avoided melodramatic pitfalls. These are the dramas that have typified the latest Golden Age of Television—*The Sopranos, Sons of Anarchy, The Wire, Deadwood* (also a period drama), *Homeland*, and my favorite, *Breaking Bad*. To watch any of them is to get an invaluable lesson on great writing with great actors at the top of their game. If you read for a show that is described like a *Bloodline* or *Breaking Bad* tone, you'll need to bring a realistic, organic style to the table.

Super-High-Stakes Drama (sometimes with Zombies or Dragons)

Yeah, I made up that category title. These are the dramas mainly about characters in some sort of power struggle, battle for survival, or other kind of desperate need. The post-apocalyptic-type drama is in this category, also shows with sci-fi or fantasy elements. The situations are usually life and death, with a high level of intensity, which demands an almost classical acting style, sometimes called "Shakespearean style." (It's no coincidence that many classically trained British actors are prominent on these shows!) Good examples are *The Walking Dead, Game of Thrones, The 100*, and *Battlestar Galactica*.

Graphic Novel/Super Hero/Sci-Fi Dramas

This is closely related to the previous category, but the characters in these shows—especially the villains—have a heightened, more melodramatic quality, and it's perfectly acceptable and even expected for them to be larger than life. Fantasy elements, supernatural powers, and a sense of dark humor are also running themes. Examples include *The Boys*, *Jessica Jones*, *Luke Cage*, *Sleepy Hollow*, *Lucifer*, *Buffy the Vampire Slayer*, *Doctor Who*, *Supernatural*, and *Gotham*. (I realize *The Walking Dead* was based on a graphic novel, but it's not in this category because the zombies don't crack jokes.)

Period Dramas

Period dramas are stories that take place during another era in history. The actors are tasked with bringing believability to their characters with the manners and style of that particular period. *Mad Men* was a wildly popular show that started a nostalgic craze for the 1950s and '60s, as well as the aforementioned *The Marvelous Mrs. Maisel*. *The Crown* is a bio-series depicting the life of Queen Elizabeth II. *Downton Abbey* was a nighttime soap following an aristocratic English family starting pre-World War I. *Turn* was a drama about Washington's spies during the Revolutionary War. One of the best recent period dramas (and also listed later in the chapter in the Gritty Drama category) is the limited series *Godless*, set in post–Civil War New Mexico and featuring a wonderful cast of actors, including a terrific Jeff Daniels as Frank Griffin.

Unique Genres

Some shows defy category. The anthology series *American Horror Story* has elements of drama, soap opera, comedy, science fiction, and horror. Another is one of my favorites, the TV show *Fargo*. On one website, it's lumped in with the dramedies, but I think that's an oversimplification. It's a character study that's both violent and darkly funny—about flawed people overreaching for money and power, which usually doesn't end well for them. The writing and acting are superb. There are so many great performances, it's hard to single one out, but I'm still amazed by Jeffrey Donovan's ability to be frightening in one moment and make me laugh in the next. His portrayal as Dodd Gerhardt, one of the sons of a North Dakota mob dynasty, is one that needs to be watched.

Reality TV

... is not part of this discussion. This book is about scripted acting, not about surviving naked in the Amazon.

Notice How Tone Can Vary Within a Genre

In all of the above categories, there are tones within tones. For example, *Gilmore Girls* has a very specific rhythm and style of dialogue, which differentiates it from the tone and style of *Monk*. The tone of *Dynasty* is distinct from the tone of *Scandal*. When you start to audition, it's important for you to know the bigger-picture genre—family drama, procedural, sketch comedy—but also the individual tone of the show if it's already on the air. Sometimes the casting breakdown will give you tone comparisons for a character (e.g., "Think Mrs. Hughes on *Downton Abbey*"), which is why it's so important for you to have a large reference base.

Tones Associated with Writers and Directors

There are also tones associated with writers and directors. I mentioned Aaron Sorkin earlier—he's considered one of our greatest writers and has written for the Broadway stage, TV, and film. His credits include *A Few Good Men*, *The Social Network*, *The West Wing*, *The Newsroom*, and *Steve Jobs*. If you've seen at least two of these, you'll notice the style—lots of clever, intelligent dialogue spoken at a fairly rapid pace. If you're reading for an Aaron Sorkin project or a project that mentions it's similar to the Aaron Sorkin style, you must be prepared to master long speeches at a quick tempo. Other examples of scribes with a unique tone are Tina Fey, who started as a writer on *SNL* and went on to create *30 Rock* and *Unbreakable Kimmy Schmidt*. Judd Apatow also started as a TV writer (*The Larry Sanders Show, Freaks and Geeks*) and is one the most dominant comedic influences behind projects like *Girls*, *Knocked Up*, *Anchorman*, *Bridesmaids*, *Trainwreck*, and many more.

It's important for you to know tones associated with certain film directors. Film is known as a director's medium because a director has a great deal of influence on the tone of the film—the look of it, rhythm, acting style, editing, humor, theme—there are so many ways a director can put their stamp on a project. Directors known for their distinctive styles are Quentin Tarantino (violence, profanity, mixed with elegant style and humor); the Coen Brothers (violence, odd characters, quirky humor); Wes Anderson (quirky characters—usually uses the same actors in his films, unique framing, whimsical set design); Martin Scorsese (gritty subject matter, specializes in Mafia themes); Michael Bay (action, explosions, over-the-top acting style). And because I think it's important that my actors know about life before 2010, I emphasize the importance of knowing about old school directors' styles—like Alfred Hitchcock, Ingmar Bergman, Akira Kurosawa, and especially Stanley Kubrick, whose films are eerie, visual masterpieces featuring jaw-dropping performances like R. Lee Ermey's in *Full Metal Jacket*.

Film Genres

While we're on the subject of film, there are common film genres that you should be familiar with: romantic comedy (aka rom-com, like *Crazy, Stupid Love* and *Crazy Rich Asians*); action adventure (*Die Hard, Raiders of the Lost Ark*); horror—which has a variety of tones from sophisticated (*The Shining*) to teen slasher (*Scream*); Marvel superhero (*Captain America* and every other movie in an octoplex now); male buddy comedy (*Superbad, 48 Hours*); female buddy comedy (*Bridesmaids, Road Trip*); epic drama (*Lord of the Rings, Dances with Wolves, The Revenant*); musicals (*Chicago, Les Miserables, La La Land*); biopics (*The Iron Lady*); and Westerns (*Unforgiven*). And there are old-school film genres that aren't necessarily part of the current mix but provide inspiration for today's films, like film noir (*The Maltese Falcon*), suspense (*Rebecca*), and melodramas (*Wuthering Heights*). (As of this publication, I booked a role playing a character from a 1940's movie in a popular current TV series. Take it from me, being a Tone Nerd pays off.)

***

The point of this seemingly endless chapter is for you to not only be adept at recognizing a particular tone but be able to execute the acting style that particular tone demands. This will be invaluable for your auditions to interpret what the producers' vision is, a shorthand you can use with directors on set, and will make you a better actor.

The best way to start is to watch everything you can. Acting is the greatest job in the world—primarily because your research involves sitting on your couch in the comfort of your home, watching great films and TV shows. So, if you're one of those cool people who is proud of saying you never watch TV, guess what? You need to start watching. If anyone complains—tell them you're working.

TONE EXERCISE — START IDENTIFYING AND STUDYING TONES

Watch a lot of film and television.

Need more explanation? This will help you understand on your own the different types of tones, (i.e., acting styles and film and TV genres), and will start a conversation that you will be having for the rest of your career in identifying the nuances of the different categories.

As a jumping-off point, here are some of the categories previously mentioned and some sample shows in each category but you will likely find many more. Your favorite show may not be listed below, but do make a note of which category it belongs in and why.

KID/TEEN COMEDY:

- *Drake & Josh*
- *iCarly*
- *Zoey 101*
- *Hannah Montana*
- *The Suite Life of Zack & Cody*
- *That's So Raven*
- *Jessie*
- *Good Luck Charlie*
- *Girl Meets World*
- *Wizards of Waverly Place*
- *Phil of the Future*
- *Even Stevens*
- *Lizzie McGuire*

CLASSIC SITCOMS — SOME SAMPLES FROM '50S–'90S

- *I Love Lucy*
- *The Honeymooners*
- *The Andy Griffith Show*
- *Gomer Pyle USMC*
- *Bewitched*

- *The Mary Tyler Moore Show*
- *The Dick Van Dyke Show*
- *The Bob Newhart Show*
- *Taxi*
- *Cheers*
- *Newhart*
- *M*A*S*H*
- *Happy Days*
- *All in the Family*
- *The Jeffersons*
- *Laverne and Shirley*
- *Good Times*
- *The Odd Couple*
- *The Brady Bunch*
- *Family Ties*
- *The Golden Girls*
- *Roseanne*
- *Married with Children*
- *Friends*
- *Frasier*
- *Full House*
- *Home Improvement*
- *Everybody Loves Raymond*
- *Absolutely Fabulous*
- *Will and Grace*
- *Martin*
- *and Seinfeld, Seinfeld, you must watch Seinfeld!*

CONTEMPORARY SITCOMS/COMEDIES

- *The Office (US and UK)*
- *The Big Bang Theory*
- *Community*
- *Modern Family*
- *Parks and Recreation*
- *It's Always Sunny in Philadelphia*
- *My Crazy Ex-Girlfriend*
- *You're the Worst*

- *Black-ish*
- *Scrubs*
- *Baskets*
- *Brooklyn Nine-Nine*
- *Glee*
- *Curb Your Enthusiasm*
- *The Good Place*
- *30 Rock*
- *Unbreakable Kimmy Schmidt*
- *Arrested Development*
- *Veep*
- *Sex and the City*
- *Master of None*
- *How I Met Your Mother*
- *Girls*
- *Barry*
- *Insecure*
- *Catastrophe*
- *The Santa Clarita Diet*
- *The Larry Sanders Show*
- *Malcolm in the Middle*
- *Fleabag*
- *Fresh Off the Boat*
- *Schitt's Creek*
- *PEN15*
- *Silicon Valley*
- *What We Do in the Shadows*
- *Ted Lasso*

CONTEMPORARY SKETCH COMEDY SHOWS

- *Saturday Night Live*
- *Key & Peele*
- *Inside Amy Schumer*
- *Broad City*
- *Portlandia*
- *A Black Lady Sketch Show*
- *I Think You Should Leave with Tim Robinson*

OTHER SKETCH COMEDY SHOWS BEFORE 2010 THAT YOU SHOULD KNOW ABOUT

- *The Carol Burnett Show*
- *Monty Python's Flying Circus*
- *The Ben Stiller Show*
- *In Living Color*
- *The State*
- *Mr. Show*
- *Your Show of Shows*
- *The Kids in the Hall*
- *SCTV*
- *Rowan and Martin's Laugh-In*
- *The Tracey Ullman Show*
- *Mad TV*
- *Upright Citizens Brigade*
- *Chappelle's Show*

DRAMEDIES (there are so, so many, I'm just listing a few here)

- *Atlanta*
- *Shameless*
- *Desperate Housewives*
- *Better Call Saul*
- *The Marvelous Mrs. Maisel*
- *Gilmore Girls*
- *Orange is the New Black*
- *Six Feet Under*
- *Glee*
- *Californication*
- *Hacks*

PROCEDURAL DRAMAS

- *Law & Order(s)*
- *NCIS(s)*
- *CSI(s)*
- *JAG*

- *Criminal Minds*
- *The Mentalist*
- *Castle*
- *The X-Files*
- *Bones*
- *The Blacklist*
- *The Closer*

DAYTIME SOAP OPERAS (currently in production as of this publication)

- *The Young and the Restless*
- *General Hospital*
- *Days of Our Lives*
- *All My Children*

PRIME-TIME SOAP OPERAS

- *Dynasty*
- *Empire*
- *Melrose Place*
- *Beverly Hills, 90210*
- *The O.C.*
- *Scandal*
- *Gossip Girl*
- *One Tree Hill*
- *Nashville*
- *The Affair*
- *Pretty Little Liars*
- *Riverdale*
- *Outer Banks*
- *Big Little Lies*

MEDICAL DRAMAS

- *Chicago Med*
- *The Resident*
- *House*
- *Grey's Anatomy*

- *ER*
- *The Good Doctor*
- *New Amsterdam*

LEGAL DRAMAS

- *The Good Wife*
- *The Good Fight*
- *Suits*
- *Boston Legal*
- *The Practice*
- *Damages*
- *How to Get Away with Murder*

FAMILY DRAMAS

- *This Is Us*
- *Parenthood*
- *Brothers and Sisters*
- *Party of Five*
- *Little House on the Prairie*
- *The Waltons*
- *Friday Night Lights*
- *The Wonder Years*

GRITTY GOLDEN-AGE DRAMAS

- *Breaking Bad*
- *Homeland*
- *Deadwood*
- *Sons of Anarchy*
- *The Wire*
- *Bloodline*
- *The Sopranos*
- 24
- *Oz*
- *The Americans*
- *Godless*

- *The People vs. OJ Simpson*
- *Fargo*
- *Narcos*
- *Ozark*
- *Euphoria*

SUPER HIGH-STAKES DRAMA (sometimes with Zombies and Dragons)

- *The Walking Dead*
- *Game of Thrones*
- *The 100*
- *Resident Evil*
- *Colony*

GRAPHIC NOVEL/SUPER HERO/SCI-FI TV SHOWS

- *Supernatural*
- *Doctor Who*
- *Gotham*
- *Buffy the Vampire Slayer*
- *Luke Cage*
- *Jessica Jones*
- *Powers*
- *Sleepy Hollow*
- *Lucifer*
- *Orphan Black*
- *Stranger Things*
- *The Boys*
- *The OA*
- *Star Trek: The Next Generation*
- *Battlestar Galactica*
- *Supergirl*
- *Marvel's Agents of SHIELD*
- *The Flash*
- *Doom Patrol*

PERIOD DRAMAS

- *Mad Men*
- *The Crown*
- *Downton Abbey*
- *Turn*
- *Boardwalk Empire*
- *Peaky Blinders*
- *Feud*
- (*Deadwood* again)

OTHER DRAMAS WORTH WATCHING FROM ALL ERAS (NOTE: the shows listed below have elements from some of the above tone categories or have their own unique tone)

- *The Handmaid's Tale*
- *American Horror Story*
- *The Twilight Zone*
- *Black Mirror*
- *Star Trek (the original from the 1960s)*
- *Rome*
- *Alias*
- *The West Wing*
- *Twin Peaks*
- *Dexter*
- *Sherlock*
- *Band of Brothers*
- *True Detective (1st season)*
- *True Blood*
- *The Newsroom*
- *Vanity Fair*
- *Succession*
- *Watchmen*
- *Billions*
- *Justified*
- *Normal People*

Watch as many shows from each category as possible, and make the following notes and observations.

DRAMAS

- What was the mood of the show? Name some descriptors (e.g., dark, quiet, tense, slow or breezy, fun, wry humor, etc.).
- Were the performances grounded (true to life) or heightened? If they were heightened, was it truthful or exaggerated?
- What was your overall impression of the dialogue? Make notes like fast-paced, witty, smart, emotionally charged, technical, realistic, theatrical, etc.
- What was your impression of the overall speaking volume and manner of delivery? Was it quiet, realistic, and underplayed or was it more overblown? If it was the latter, was it due to an urgent situation or because the show's style was melodramatic?
- What was the color palette of the show? Notice if it was shot with a themed color, like sepia, gray, or dark teal (like *The Handmaid's Tale*). The color palette is an important factor of the mood and tone of the show.
- Make a note if any of the dramas have humorous or lighter moments. How did that affect your impression of the show? How would that impact your choices if you were to audition for the show?

COMEDIES

- Watch comedies from different eras, from the 1950s to the present. What are some of the differences in jokes, characters, speaking volume, physicality? Do any of the old shows make you laugh, and if so, why? How do the newer comedies differ?
- Watch one of the Kid/Teen comedies listed. Note the exaggeration or the "bigness" of the acting. What were the stakes of the situation? Did the actor make it truthful? How would you do it truthfully and match the comedic tone of the show?
- Pick a line that made you laugh, and make a note of why it was funny. Was it a well-written joke or did it make you laugh because it came from the character's behavior, or both?

- On that note, observe how the actors get laughs. Are they mugging for the camera—trying to make you laugh—or committed to the situation?
- Watch one of the more recent comedies, like *Parks and Recreation*, *Modern Family*, or *The Office*. Note the difference in tone and behavior to the earlier sitcoms. Even when the character's point of view is absurd, how do the actors make it truthful? (Hint: Notice Dwight Schrute from *The Office* in his I Believe moments!)

This chapter isn't intended to be the last word on tone, and everyone's going to have an opinion (*Better Call Saul*'s a dramedy?) But I hope it will set you on the path to paying attention and identifying tone for yourself. When you're doing your research watching film and television, have a strong vision of yourself on the screen. That will set the perfect tone for your working actor career.

THE STEVEN HILL EXERCISES

FOR EPISODIC/PROCEDURAL TONE

I always say to students if you want to be an actor, watch other actors, make up your mind about whether you like that or whether it conveys the story to you because only that way can you learn.
—Dame Judi Dench

My husband enjoys watching the original *Law & Order* reruns because he's a big fan of the "Lennie-isms"—the witty comments Detective Lennie Briscoe makes while investigating a crime—like "You probably know you have the right to remain silent. Why don't you use it?"

I didn't watch *Law & Order* when it was originally on in the '90s and early 2000s because I assumed it was just another formulaic cop show. But during periods of gym-avoidance, I started watching with my husband and began to appreciate this show—not only because it's entertaining but for the lessons it provided about acting in the Procedural Tone. There's a particular rhythm to the dialogue according to the type of scene—from the cops on the crime scene to the interrogation of witnesses and suspects to the attorneys discussing the details of a case behind closed doors to the climactic courtroom scenes. The characters are portrayed as hard-working and serious about getting the job done, and yet they sometimes use wry humor in their darkest moments. Without mentioning it, you sense they get very little sleep, survive on junk food and coffee, sometimes a little bourbon tipple, and they work into the wee hours of the morning to solve a case. The show is shot in somber colors, which also adds to the mood and enhances the acting style.

The original *Law & Order* cast consisted of fine actors, many with Broadway pedigrees. The late Jerry Orbach was wonderful as Briscoe, Jesse L. Martin as Ed Green, S. Epatha Merkerson as Anita Van Buren, and in later seasons Sam Waterston as Assistant District Attorney Sam McCoy.

And then there was this guy who played District Attorney Adam Schiff. He looked like someone they picked up from the Manhattan Criminal Courthouse and dumped on the set. He was rumpled, unaffected, and always in quiet command, rarely raising his voice. That was my introduction to the great actor Steven Hill.

If you look up Steven Hill's credits on IMDb (The Internet Movie Database), you'll see he's had an interesting career dating back to 1949. He was also one of the founding members of the Actor's Studio. As a fan of the realism school of acting, I found him fascinating to watch. His multitasking while discussing a case with his colleagues, his little bits of business (or what I call Secondary Activity) as he was processing information, his self-control even during testy debates with his staff. How he would sit and listen, knitting pieces of information together, guiding his staff to solutions, sometimes at the end of a long day when his eyestrain was palpable. You forgot he was an actor because you never caught him acting.

I wanted my students to be able to embody this same type of effortlessness because I knew it would elevate the quality of their work. If they could master this acting style, they would understand the acting tone of many episodic series—real, grounded, underplayed—and it would give them a better shot of booking roles on these types of shows.

I decided the best way to impart this lesson was for them to watch an Adam Schiff scene to observe Steven Hill in action, and then to mimic what they saw in order to experience what this tone feels like. "*Why would I mimic another actor—wouldn't that lead to bad acting?*" The mimicking part is important because this type of real behavior, of seemingly doing nothing, feels strange until the actor begins to trust it. Think of it like taking a lesson from a tennis pro—you observe, you imitate, you integrate it into your muscle memory and eventually develop your own style.

Adam Schiff's demeanor on the show is very much the epitome of the Procedural Tone—a professional focused on solving a crime or figuring out a case. You will also notice how Mode of Being, Body Language, and Do Your Job! come into play. The Steven Hill exercise incorporates all of the above.

When you do the first part of the exercise, which is to watch as many as possible but at least one of the Adam Schiff/Steven Hill scenes, I want you to take particular notice of the Secondary Activity he does naturally, like adjusting his tie, fiddling with a pen, shuffling paperwork, picking lint off his jacket. You may think that's silly, but I suggest you notice when great actors do this instinctively. They understand that human beings don't freeze stiffly while talking, but we are constantly engaged in absent-minded activity. Just adding those bits of behavior consciously can make an inexperienced actor look like a seasoned professional.

Sadly, Steven Hill passed away in Manhattan the summer of 2016 when I started writing this book. It would be a great testament to him if you learned something from the legacy of work he left behind. If you end up even a fraction as good as he was, you'll have come a long way.

The Steven Hill exercise — part one

YOU'LL NEED: A TV set or laptop and possibly a cable subscription. Or spend $1.99 apiece (as of this writing) and buy one or several *Law & Order* episodes on Amazon. Watch at least one of Adam Schiff's scenes in the original *Law & Order* series (the one that began production in 1990 with no extra initials). He's in the first ten seasons (229 episodes), so if you happen to catch a rerun on TV, he'll likely be in it. I've already curated some of my favorite episodes from the first two seasons with the timestamps of his more noteworthy scenes in the Appendix (even though he's in many more than noted), and I highly recommend you watch as many of them as possible.

After watching, make the following observations.

- What was his primary activity? (Examples: listening, problem solving, writing notes, etc.) In what situations do you find yourself involved in the same types of activity?
- What, if any, was the Secondary Activity? (Examples: fiddling with a piece of clothing, tapping reading glasses or a pencil, etc.)
- What Body Language did you notice? How was his posture? How did other movements or gestures depict his state of mind?
- If you were to guess, did the scene take place first thing in the morning, in the afternoon, early evening, or late night? Note factors like the light in the room, energy level, signs of fatigue.
- What is his status in relation to the other people in the room? How does he portray that status? Does he throw his weight around or operate with a quiet confidence? Does that give you any ideas about the choices you might make when you audition for or play a similar role?
- Take note of how he listens to his colleagues. Do you see him process what they're saying?

- How would you describe his character traits and Mode of Being? (Hint: use descriptive words and phrases, like "Calm Problem Solver" or "Battle-Weary Survivor.") In what situation(s) do you find yourself in the same mode?

THE STEVEN HILL EXERCISE — PART TWO

You'll need: To transcribe—aka write out— at least one scene from the original *Law & Order* series and at least one or more actors for your scene partners. It's also highly recommended you record yourself.

> BIG NOTE: Want to know how to transcribe a scene from a film or TV show? I turn on the "Closed Captioning" feature and write the dialogue as it appears onscreen.

This is where it gets interesting. You will perform one of the scenes and cast other actors in the other roles (usually Ben and Paul). Whether you are male, female, or nonbinary, you will play Adam.

Now that you have a script, even after seeing the scene, note how easy or difficult it was for you to adopt this particular tone. In class I've made the following observations after the first pass.

Energy Level and Body Language — In watching these episodes I've purposely mentioned that you observe time of day and fatigue levels. The actors bring dimension to their characters and tell the story through their body language. Note how you are aware of their fatigue, the long hours worked just by a sigh, a slump in the shoulders, a rub of the forehead or eyes. Those small, organic gestures speak volumes about their inner life and the day they've had, the frustration of a particular case, the years of doing battle every day.

The biggest mistake my newer actors make is to completely ignore these very important cues and approach the scene as if they've just guzzled a gallon of coffee. Instead of battle weary, they're bright and shiny, like a cub reporter on the first day of the job!

Acting coaches develop certain shortcuts, and here is mine for this particular issue: the headache. I've seen remarkable transformations with that one simple adjustment.

If you fell into this very common trap, take a moment now and imagine a headache. If you're a common headache sufferer, use your muscle memory to recall the spot where you feel it most—behind your eyes, your temple, the top of your head? I'm not a headache sufferer, but I find the image of eyestrain or a hangover particularly effective. Close your eyes and let it intensify so that it becomes real. Be patient—this works.

Now, keeping that headache, do the scene again. Let the headache affect your energy, your pace. Take a moment, and rub the affected area as you're talking.

If you recorded this second take, notice the difference it made in your performance. Every time we've made this adjustment in class, it's elevated the work exponentially.

Do Your Job! — In the Do Your Job! chapter, you experienced how using your Knowledge Base gave you confidence, even with scripts and dialogue that you had no previous experience with. Sometimes actors in their first pass doing the Steven Hill exercise forget this very important aspect. The character Adam Schiff, like many other characters in these procedural dramas, have been at their job for a while and even when the chips are down, exude a sense of career history, knowledge, and confidence.

If you found yourself feeling uncomfortable and unconfident during your Adam scene, go back to describing your job in minute detail. If you work with coworkers, recall any verbal exchange you have had with them, no matter how mundane. Get that feeling back in your body of knowing what you know. Mimic Adam's body language—he's almost always relaxed, even during the tensest exchanges. Now do the scene again and record it. Feel and see the difference?

Secondary Activity — Every now and again, Adam will have a small bit of organic behavior while he's discussing a case with a colleague that brings even more reality and dimension to the scene. If you found yourself stiffly saying lines and exhibiting other robotic behavior, I coach my actors to find secondary activity that grounds and relaxes them in a scene.

Some examples of secondary behavior you can incorporate while doing your dialogue:

- Wiping your eyeglasses on your shirt
- Adjusting your watchband
- Fiddling with a scrap of paper
- Picking a piece of lint off your shirt
- Doodling on a notepad
- Loosening or adjusting your tie or another piece of clothing

(Start observing your behavior and find your own.)

In a perfect world, every actor is so relaxed on stage that these little bits of activity come naturally. But with new actors, such is usually not the case. Only after they're coached to add this behavior in these scenes, the actor begins to understand how physically loose—and human—they can be. Even if Adam doesn't do a bit of Secondary Activity—and quite often he just sits and talks or listens—to do this while doing his dialogue is extremely effective.

BIG NOTE: When you're learning this tool, remember to not lay on the Secondary Activity so thick it becomes distracting. Think of it as a subtle seasoning you're adding to your acting stew.

Mode of Being, Character Description and Script Approach—This is an extremely important lesson about approaching a script and incorporating the Mode of Being of a character into your interpretation.

If you transcribed a scene, you've already watched the performance and seen Steven Hill's interpretation. Forget that for a moment and just look at the lines of dialogue. I've paraphrased a few typical phrases.

- "Yeah, what are you talking about?"
- "What's that got to do with anything?"
- "Can't anyone around here stick together for five seconds?"

Imagine the assumptions a new actor would make about that dialogue. Most would fall into the trap of making it dramatic, confrontational, *actory*!

But given everything you now know about Procedural Tone, about energy level and time of day, how would that change your interpretation?

Now let's add Character Description and Mode of Being. Let's say the character was described as:

Adam Schiff (40–60) Seasoned District Attorney. Been at the job for years. Seen everything, and nothing much surprises or rattles him. Rarely loses his temper or command. A confident leader guiding his staff in solving problems.

You've had the advantage of watching his scenes and describing his character traits. Now translate those into one or several Modes of Being. Here are some possibilities.

- Problem Solver
- Wise Leader
- Battle-Weary Survivor
- Listener
- Thinker
- Cool Boss

Using everything you've learned from watching Steven Hill and what we've discussed in this chapter, now apply that to the dialogue above. Solving a problem. Thinking and listening. It's the end of a twelve-hour day, so ... weary. How does that change your approach?

After doing these Steven Hill exercises in class, my students noticed a vast improvement on their scene work and auditions for this type of Procedural Tone. Watch how you improve and how much you can learn just by observing an excellent actor at the top of his game.

IMPROVISATION

Life is improvisation.
—Tina Fey

It's a lifetime ago. I'm in my twenties, living in a dingy studio apartment off Olympic Boulevard in Los Angeles. My dented Datsun B210 is parked on the street, wheezing fumes and leaking oil like an incontinent drunk. I'm lying on the couch, staring at the TV with glazed eyes, trying to forget the humiliation of yet another bad audition, but it replays over and over in my head—a waking nightmare on an endless loop.

When I say *bad audition*, I don't mean cute-movie bad, where the ingenue blows a line, giggles, and gets the starring role. I mean bad as in a sweaty, twitchy, stuttering ball of goo, blurting out something awkwardly off-putting to the casting director right before taking a perfectly good script and transforming it into a pile of pig vomit. My auditions weren't just bad, they were epically awful.

So, when I mentioned earlier in the book that in the beginning of my career, I sucked, I wasn't exaggerating or feigning humility. As soon as I walked into an audition, my nerves would paralyze me, and I felt like I was floating above my body, watching myself stumble below. Failure has a strong gravitational pull, and for the longest time, I tried and failed to break free from its grip. What saved me at that point in my life wasn't an acting class—it was comedy improvisation, first as a student with The Groundlings and later as a performer with ComedySportz in Los Angeles.

While doing improv, I experienced freedom on stage that I had never felt in a scripted play. I was with other actors, creating something out of thin air that sometimes soared and sometimes flopped, but that was the exciting thing about it—you never knew or cared about the outcome. The only thing that mattered was being in the moment, creating a character on the spot, feeling fully committed and alive. It brought back the same joy I felt playing "drama" after school with my childhood friends.

This feeling of freedom also translated to my auditions, and I don't think it was a coincidence that I started having better success with callbacks and bookings. I brought that same looseness into the audition room, bringing more of an improvisational feel to scripted material, and now the casting director or producer was my friend and teammate. It was all beginning to click—finally.

Cut to several years later in my classroom in St. Petersburg. My students were composed of a range of personality types and experience, but just about everyone had this in common: they were nervous on stage. My solution? Throw comedy improv at 'em.

I've learned that actors are terrified of improv until they start to appreciate the thrill of having little to work with besides the other actors and an audience suggestion. Getting laughs also helps, since most of the improv we do is comedy-based. I believe the comedy part is important, even if you want to spend the rest of your life doing *Hamlet*. A well-rounded actor is an actor who can do comedy.

I introduced improv exercises to my classes soon after I began teaching, and it's become an invaluable part of my curriculum. Starting the class with an improv exercise gets the blood flowing and the synapses firing. Improvisation trains my students to listen and be in the present moment. Everyone gets stage time, and the class starts on a positive note with laughter and energy. As a result, the students who had been struggling with scripted material found their confidence doing improv, and consequently their scene work improved. All of the power I found in improv several years earlier was now showing up in my actors. Some fell so in love with it that they started their own performing group. Ah, the circle of life!

My belief in improvisation skills isn't just a personal quirk—there's also a big-picture reason. Almost every director I've talked to prefers actors who are comfortable with improv. Sometimes a spontaneous, improvised moment in an audition will win a job. Sometimes these are "mistakes" where the actor forgets their lines or some other mishap. An actor trained in improv knows how to turn these unplanned moments into golden opportunities!

Many great moments in movies were improvised, not just in comedies but in drama as well—perhaps most famously Robert DeNiro's "You talkin' to me?" riff looking at himself in the mirror in *Taxi Driver.* Some movies were almost completely improvised, like *Blue Valentine*. More and more I hear stories about actors given the direction in an audition or on a set to use the script as a guideline but to make the words their own or "have fun with it." My actors are prepared for these types of scenarios. Actors who don't have improv training are not.

If you've completed the other exercises in this book, you've already done some improv without realizing it, even if the exercise started with a script. The second takes of the Personal Scene and the Everyday Scene and extended Hot Person exercise had improvisation. The Hot Person Confrontation and Intervention were improvised interactions, I Believe was an improvised speech, and the Mode of Being exercises are all improvisation. The Body Language Personality and Character Dances are two of our favorite improv exercises to start the class. The Build A Place exercise is your first taste of improv "space work" dealing with invisible objects. So, if you think you can't improvise, think again. There are no excuses going forward.

There are many wonderful books dedicated to improvisation, written by masters of the art, and I'm not trying to compete with them. I am offering some of my favorite exercises that we do in class that incorporate the most basic improv rules and techniques, as well as some exercises that I've developed specifically to enhance and strengthen certain skills. Have fun playing!

IMPROV EXERCISE #1 — LEARN THE RULES OF IMPROV

There are basic rules in improvisation that must be followed, or else the improv game will implode, and body parts will scatter to all corners of the stage. Okay, not quite, but you do need to learn the rules when you are a beginning improviser. You will find that if you or your fellow actors ignore these rules, the scene will fall apart. But if you follow the rules and learn to trust them, your scene has the potential to be wonderful, even if you're a newbie. The more you practice, the more these rules will become second nature.

RULE #1 — SCENES ARE BUILT BY OFFERS

An offer is an element spoken by a player that adds information to a scene. Examples of offers include naming yourself, the other actor, the place, what you're wearing, your profession, and anything else that adds information to the scene.

You build a scene, one offer at a time, collaborating with your fellow actor(s).

An example of offers in a scene:

Actor A
"*Mrs. Richards*, it's good to see you again!" (Named her, indicating an existing relationship.)

Actor B
"Yes, *Johnny*, welcome back to *detention*." (Added information naming him and where they are.)

Actor A
"I love *what you've done with the room*." (Added information about the detention room.)

Actor B
"Yes, I added a *dunce chair* in the corner just for *you* ..." (Added a juicy bit of information that not only refers to an object but signifies that Johnny is a bad boy!)

Notice how this was an *established relationship*, rather than two strangers. Whenever possible, have a history with the other person on stage; it always leads to a stronger scene. Also notice every offer was received with a "yes and," so that information was added. Which brings us to the next rule.

RULE #2 — ALWAYS SAY "YES, AND"

That means **Yes**, you are accepting your scene partner's offer, **And** adding information. An example of blocking an offer, which results in bad improv:

Actor A — "I love your hat!"

Actor B — "I'm not wearing a hat."

Because of fear or inexperience, many new improvisers will become naysayers on stage. Actor A started with the offer: "I love your hat!" If Actor B says "Yes, and ..." he's allowing potential magical things to happen. For example:

Actor A
"I love your hat!"

Actor B
"Yes, it's great being pope for a day!"

Actor B added the information that it's not just a hat, it's a pope's mitre. That opens the scene up to many possibilities—it can now track how Actor A became pope for a day or a myriad of other absurdities, all from just saying Yes. (By the way, you don't literally have to say "Yes, And" in the scene, as illustrated above. The "And" implies you've added information.)

RULE #3 — MAKE STATEMENTS RATHER THAN ASKING QUESTIONS!

It's always a stronger choice to know things than to be the person on stage who knows nothing, unless you've been given the suggestion of being an amnesiac. Most new improvisers are afraid of making offers and adding information. Don't be concerned about the "right" choice—just make a choice, and trust that the scene will unfold with the help of your scene partners, usually better than you anticipated. The sooner you get in that habit, the quicker your improvised scenes will improve.

This is a typical non-offer made by a novice improviser. The suggestion we asked for was a location, and "bar" was given by the audience.

Actor A (entering, talking to the bartender) — "Who are you? What do you serve here? What kind of place is this?"

That puts all of the weight of the scene onto Actor B, the bartender. Actor A made no offers and is contributing nothing to the scene, which now has very little potential to go anywhere.

A potentially better scene:

Actor A (entering, talking to the bartender) — "Hey Harry. Gimme the usual."

Actor B — "Sure thing Sylvia. Vodka chocolate chip shake coming right up!"

See what they did? They not only added information, they established a previous *relationship*, which is gold in improv. The actors made strong choices of knowing each other and having a history, plus the information of Sylvia's favorite drink. Now they can continue with the origin of that odd drink, their relationship, or a number of other possible scenarios.

RULE #4 — AVOID THE "EWW" FACTOR

I have to mention this because I see this a lot with new improvisers. I've named it the "EWW" Factor and it manifests in these types of ways on stage: "I don't like you." "Get away from me." "You're ugly." "Shut up." "Get out of my bar." "Stop talking." This angry and uncooperative tone that some new actors adopt is a result of fear and inexperience, and as you can probably guess, shuts down the scene beyond repair. I always have the actors start the scene again and coach them to first of all, be happy! And then use "Yes, And" responses, which then gets the scene back on track. Remember, good improv is about taking care of and lifting up your scene partner(s), which leads me to the next rule.

RULE #5 — GIVE AND TAKE

Watching experienced improvisers in performance is like watching an expert tennis match—one player hits the ball (makes an offer), and the other player hits the ball back (accepts the offer, adds information). There is trust that once the offer is made, it will be returned in kind. This back-and-forth exchange, or Give and Take, can add up to a brilliantly improvised scene where both partners have equal share in the scene's success.

The opposite is true when a new improviser takes the stage and talks nonstop, not making any offers or allowing any other actor to get a word in edgewise. This might be somewhat palatable if the monologuing actor is saying anything interesting, but that's rarely the case. If this happens in class, I stop the scene and gently remind the actor they are violating the sacred rule of Give and Take. They're coached to make or accept an offer and then let the other actor or actors participate in the scene.

I believe this issue is caused by nerves, fear of losing control, and lack of trust. Part of being a good improviser and a good actor is understanding that any scene, whether written or improvised, is a collaboration. Even if your *characters* are at odds, the *actors* must approach a scene in the spirit of cooperation.

RULE #6 — LOCATION AND SPACE WORK

In the Place chapter, you did the Build A Place and Activities in an Environment exercises. Now you'll see how they will ground you in your improvised scenes.

One of my biggest pet peeves during our improv scenes is when my actors get a location, something juicy like "NASA Mission Control" and act the entire scene in the middle of the stage like talking heads—not moving or incorporating the possibilities of activity in their given environment. The point of getting a location suggestion is using the location—not talking about it.

In improv, one of the most common audience suggestions is location. When you're given a location, picture all of the details of that location, including the furnishings and objects within. If you're given the location "bar" like the example in Rule #3, one of the actors should jump into the role of bartender and immediately start an activity that a bartender would logically do, like wipe down the space bar with a space rag or put away space glasses like we did in the Place Exercise #4. If the location is "beach," one of the actors might start the scene unfurling a beach towel or climbing a lifeguard's tower. You can create a fascinating scene without saying a word by mining all of the possibilities your location offers, and the audience will eat it up.

The same goes with space work. When I watched an Upright Citizens Brigade show in New York City a few years back, one of the actors established he was a janitor in a location and began sweeping the floor with a space broom. When another character entered, he rested his chin on the "broom" and carried on a conversation. It brought the house down.

When you start to do improv and follow the location and space work rules, this will automatically improve your scene work and auditions. You may choose not to do space work in a live audition, but your experience and activity playing a receptionist in an improv scene will inform your behavior auditioning for a role as a receptionist for a film or TV show. Those nuances you discovered will still come through.

IMPROV EXERCISE #2 — *WHOSE LINE IS IT, ANYWAY?*

For this exercise, you'll need a TV or laptop.

Before I started performing improv, I learned a lot by watching great improvisers on stage. The TV show *Whose Line Is It, Anyway?* is a great show to study the best improvisers in the business, like Ryan Stiles, Wayne Brady, Colin Mochrie, and my friend Brad Sherwood. A classic episode features Richard Simmons as a guest improviser in a game called "Living Sceneries," but there are many more examples on YouTube and TV. Watch as much as possible, and you'll laugh and learn at the same time.

IMPROV EXERCISE #3 — "YES, AND"

You need: At least three players, but the game should be played with as many people as possible.

This exercise is taught in almost every Improv 101 class and is a drill to get the actors accustomed to always adding information, or in Improv Speak, to say "Yes, And ..."

In my classes, we usually start with a storybook title suggestion, something that is similar to a children's fable but more absurd, like "The Frog and the Crouton" or "The Adventures of the Little Red Pickle."

The players will stand in a circle, and the first player, chosen at random, will start the story usually with one sentence, for example: "Once upon a time there lived a frog on a lake." The player to their left will then add their contribution: "Yes, and the lake was filled with runoff from a neighboring bakery." The next player will add: "Yes, and the neighboring bakery specialized in parmesan-flavored bread," and so on. Every player builds on what the previous player has offered, to continue the story. Depending on how many players there are in a group, the story can circle around several times and go off on unexpected tangents by the time it comes back to you a second or third time.

Saying "Yes, And" helps you develop the habit of acknowledging the information you're receiving and adding your own information. The best "Yes, Ands" in this exercise offer a detailed nugget of information ("the neighboring bakery specialized in parmesan-flavored bread"). You will notice it works best to relinquish your preconceived notion of where the story should go and stay in the moment to support the story. This exercise illustrates how improv is a group effort and reinforces the notion that you must work together as a team, adding information for a successful outcome.

Improv exercise #4 — Story Story

Needs: Four to six players and one "conductor."

This is another exercise taught in many Improv 101 classes and one that we did in performance in ComedySportz as an elimination game. It's the same principle as "Yes, And," in that you're using the same listening and adding-information skills, but it goes much quicker, so the level of difficulty is greater.

The conductor gets a suggestion for a story title from the audience along the same lines as the children's fable in "Yes, And." The players stand in a line on stage, and the conductor kneels in front of them with their back to the audience. The conductor points to the first player in any random order they choose, and the first player will begin the story. While the conductor has their finger pointed at the player, the player must continue to talk until the conductor switches and points to another player. The beginning of this game has a more leisurely pace—each player can get out at least one or two sentences of the story, but as the game progresses the conductor makes quicker switches, so sometimes the players are cut off after one word or even after one syllable.

Ideally the players are listening to each other and following the conductor's direction so closely that they continue the story seamlessly, for example:

Player A: "Once upon a time, there was a swan who lived in the forest. She" (Conductor switches to)

Player B: "had beautiful white wings because she bathed herself every day in" (Conductor switches to)

Player C: "organic, grass-fed milk ..." and so on.

In the elimination part of this, if a player hesitates, repeats a word just said, fumbles, or just doesn't make any sense, they're eliminated. This gets really fun when the conductor is making quick switches, sometimes in mid-syllable. If a player is thrown that curve but can continue seamlessly, it adds to the fun of the game. For example:

Player A: "The swan had" (Conductor switches to)

Player B: "to face" (Conductor switches to)

Player C: "the con-" (Conductor switches to)

Player A: "-ga line and dance ..."

Like every other improv game, this one takes practice, but as you develop your listening and adding information skills, it's a great game for class and for performance.

Improv exercise #5 — Changing Emotions

Needs at least four people — two players and two emotion callers.

Sometimes an improv scene can start to founder, and the actors might start to feel stuck. This exercise is another staple of Improv 101 classes and demonstrates how extreme emotional changes can move a scene along while getting big laughs.

For this exercise, two emotion callers will ask the audience for several emotions, enough for them to fill a few columns on a pad of paper. Two players take the stage, and each player is assigned to one of the callers. The two players then start a scene with an audience suggestion of either a location, a relationship, or even a first line of dialogue.

Shortly after the scene begins, one of the callers yells "Freeze!" Both players freeze. The caller then yells one of the emotions on the list, and the actor assigned to them must now proceed with the scene in that emotion until another one is called for them. The other player continues in neutral until their caller provides an emotion for them.

For example, the location is an ice-cream store.

Player A:
"I'd like an ice cream, please."

Player B:
"Certainly, we have chocolate and vanilla today."

Caller for A:
"Freeze! Anger!"

Player A:
"CHOCOLATE! I HATE CHOCOLATE! IT GIVES ME ZITS! YOU'RE TRYING TO GIVE ME ZITS, AREN'T YOU?"

Player B: "
No, ma'am, I'm just trying to ..."

Caller for B:
"Freeze! Sadness!"

Player B:
"I'm just trying to find someone to love me. (Breaks down and weeps.) I need a hug!"

When the callers freeze the players, the players must give each other space for the emotional adjustment. If Caller A freezes Player A, Player B must allow Player A to be the first one to continue with the scene with their new emotion.

BIG NOTE: When the Players are given the emotions, they need to commit to them 1,000 percent, in other words, over the top. It's improv and absurd, and the commitment adds to the absurdity and the comedy.

Since the callers are controlling the scene, they must be in tune with the rhythm of the scene and the emotions. A good caller can time the emotions at just the right moment for maximum comedic impact.

The players can also help the callers by giving them obvious pauses to jump in. A typical example is:

Player A:
"Vanilla ice cream makes me feel so very ..." (thinks and pauses)

Caller A:
"Freeze! Sexy!"

Player A:
"... horny."

I love this exercise because it lets the actors experience how effective it is to let emotions change the course of a scene—how effortless the dialogue becomes just by committing to the emotion. Going big in comedy improv is very freeing, and this freedom translates to your other acting work.

IMPROV EXERCISE #6 — REPLAY

Needs two to four players.

One of my favorite exercises in class and in performance is any version of a Replay game. The Replay game's structure is very simple—the actors do a minute-long neutral scene, meaning no big emotional adjustment and usually in an ordinary location, like a hair salon. The dialogue should be very bland, because it will change later. In ComedySportz, we would do this with as many as four players in a scene but it's easier done with two in class.

Example of the neutral scene:

Player A: "
Hello, Charlene, sorry I'm late for my appointment."

Player B:
"No problem, Doris. I'm still sharpening my scissors."

Player A:
"I think I want to go shorter today."

Player B:
"Ooh, good idea!" etc.

One of the Replay options is Emotional Replay, where the players will repeat the neutral scene but are given a different emotion each time the scene is replayed. Both of the players will use the same emotion for the scene, and part of the fun is how the lines slightly change according to the emotion. For example, if the given emotion for the replay is PMS:

Player A:
"Hello, Charlene, sorry I'm late for my appointment. (Breaks down.) Turns out something else is late too."

Player B:
"No problem, Doris, I've got cramps. I'm sharpening my scissors to get into this box of chocolate." (Makes stabbing gestures.)

Player A:
"I was thinking about going shorter today, but I'm so bloated, I'm afraid it'll make me look fat."

Player B:
"Oh, honey, I feel fat too." (They both break down and hug each other.)

In other versions of this exercise, the Replays can be a movie genre, director, or music style. Imagine what the neutral scene above would be like replayed as a Michael Bay action film, a horror film, or a Western. And then as a rap song, country ballad, or opera duet?

Because I'm so big on my students knowing tone, I've started doing Replays using tone genres of TV shows. The neutral scene can be replayed as a daytime soap, a Disney kids' show, *The Walking Dead*, or any of the categories mentioned in the Tone chapter.

IMPROV EXERCISE #7 — EXPERT

No minimum number of players required.

In my studio, we do this in both the adult and the kids' classes—it's especially a favorite with the kids.

In the Do Your Job! chapter, we talked about using your Knowledge Base to convincingly play a character who's an expert in a field you know nothing about. This improv game uses the same concept. As a warm-up, we start with an actor giving us a lecture about something that they have a great deal of knowledge or experience with—whether it's scrambling eggs or rebuilding an engine.

They are then given an unrelated topic that they must now assume the role of expert and give a lecture on the spot. It's a given you won't know about the topic, whether it's reality based, like oil painting, or off the wall, like gnome hunting or burping: "The greatest oil paintings have been made from Valvoline." The key is to use the same Knowledge Base mode and deliver the lecture with confidence, no matter how erroneous or absurd the actual facts are. If you can master this exercise talking extemporaneously about a topic about which you have zero knowledge, you will be able to handle scripted material with even more confidence.

IMPROV EXERCISE #8 — IMPROVISE IN CHARACTER

No minimum players needed—you can even do this alone.

This is similar to the Mode of Being exercise, in that you are talking and behaving in character, either one you're improvising or working on from a script. This is a great exercise if you are working on a role and want to dive deeper into their thoughts and emotions.

Sit or stand as your character would. This is an opportunity to explore their body language. Would they stand tall and erect? Slump in a chair? To explore their physicality, take a few moments and either walk around the room or sit in a chair as they would.

Now, start a sentence with you as the human being you're embodying, saying "I Believe" or "I Need." You also have the option to start with "I Feel" or "I Want." Don't preplan what you're going to say; just start with those two words and trust what will unfold.

As an improv exercise, the character organically emerges as soon as you begin with one of the "I" statements. Just begin talking, and trust that will happen—the results are amazing! It's also an extremely powerful way to explore a character that you're working on and can give you more dimension than the script provides.

PRAGMATIC ACTOR TAKEAWAYS

- For all roles, especially the smaller costar type roles moving the story along, determine if your character has a specific Mode of Being.
- Given your information about the character, (e.g., their personality, status, activity, emotional state), explore their Body Language, especially upon entrance and throughout the scene.
- If your character has a Professional Mode of Being, use your Knowledge Base to seamlessly embody confidence and competence.
- Commit to studying tone for the rest of your career as a working actor!
- Use the Steven Hill exercises to deepen your understanding of relaxation and realism, not only for the Professional Mode of Being and the Procedural Tone but also for similar types of roles.
- Take a comedy improv class and use basic improv skills to bring looseness and spontaneity to your auditions and your acting work!

PART FOUR
THE WORKING ACTOR

Bit by bit, putting it together
Piece by piece, only way to make a work of art
Every moment makes a contribution
Every little detail plays a part
Having just a vision's no solution
Everything depends on execution
Putting it together, that's what counts
—Stephen Sondheim, *Putting It Together* from
Sunday in the Park with George

YOU'RE WANTED ON THE SET!

I think there's a difference between a working actor, a movie star, and a celebrity. They're all three different things.
—Chadwick Boseman

Congratulations, you've made it to Part Four—The Working Actor! The Act ALIVE exercises in the previous chapters are designed to prepare you for the real work of doing scenes, like pummeling the heavy bag prepares a champion boxer or practicing scales readies a concert pianist. As elite artists and athletes rely on coaching throughout their careers to perform at peak levels, the guidance in this section will coach you to master your scene work at a professional level. Now the fun begins!

The chapters in this last section contain suggested strategies to use your newfound knowledge for every role you tackle, whether it be a scene in class or an audition for a major studio project. The art of creating a character is like painting—you start with an outline or rough sketch, and as you continue your process, all the color, nuance, and details begin to emerge. But unlike the *Mona Lisa*, your masterpiece has a beating heart and a noble purpose: to tell a story that can potentially entertain, educate, and uplift us.

"Okay," I hear you saying, "you're making this sound really easy. But I read your whole book—all sixteen chapters and forty-four exercises plus improvisation. That's a lot. Are you expecting me to magically know which exercises to use?"

It may take some practice, but the more material you work on, the stronger your instincts will be as to what will make you jump off the page. Some of my tools I recommend you use all of the time (hello, Hot Person!) and others only as needed. If you were cast as Elsa in *Frozen*, would you use the information in Do Your Job!? Uh, no. That's what I'm talking about.

Remember your ultimate goal—to make your work truthful and spontaneous. Your job is to take words from a page and use them to embody a three-dimensional human being. To make us feel like we're eavesdropping on a real event. Whether you used one tool, several tools, or just rolled out of bed to nail it, trust it when you've achieved it. This isn't like math, where you need to prove how you did it. All we need to do is believe you. Your feedback will be that wonderful phone call, "Great news, you're wanted on the set!"

THE BIG PICTURE

The script, I always believe, is the foundation of everything.
—Ewan McGregor

You're picking up a script for the first time. Your adrenaline is pumping, and all you want to do is jump straight to your character's lines—just those lines and nothing else. After all, it's four pages, and the audition is tomorrow. You've got a lot of memorizing to do, plus, you've got to get to the dry cleaners before they close. Oh, and a manicure. And. And. And ....

I get it. I've been there. So, I can tell you from experience: Stop. Take a deep breath. The most effective thing you can do right now to maximize your preparation is to get a sense of the Big Picture of the project—the story you are telling, and how your character fits into that story. This is always the research you should do before *every* audition, whether it be one line for a TV show, a supporting character in a play, or the lead of a film. It won't take long, and it will increase your chances of getting cast in the role. (By the way, the word is cast, not *casted*. That's not a word. Saying it is like plastering a big ROOKIE sign on your back.)

When you first get your script, read it several times but at least once. Ask yourself the following questions.

What is the Story?

What is the overall story—or plot—of the film, play, or TV show, in one or two sentences? You may have to summarize on your own, or you may have been provided with a synopsis like the following.

Harold & Kumar Go to White Castle: Nerdy accountant Harold and his irrepressible friend, Kumar, get stoned watching television, watch a commercial for White Castle, and set out on a quest for a burger.

David Makes Man is an hourlong television episodic centered on a 14-year-old prodigy trying to find a way out of poverty for himself, his mother, and younger brother. He is torn between life on his boyhood streets or the higher education that may lead to a better life.

CSI: Crime Scene Investigation is an hourlong television episodic following a forensics team of investigators as they analyze physical evidence to solve crimes.

Schitt's Creek follows the misadventures of the formerly wealthy Rose family, whose only remaining asset—and new home—is the town of Schitt's Creek, which they had previously bought as a joke.

Robot's Revenge: A rogue robot created as a college science project hunts down its inventors and wreaks havoc on the university. (I made this one up. Call me, Netflix.)

Note that whether these are preexisting projects or one I made up, there are clues of tone in the synopses. ("Nerdy" and "irrepressible" character descriptions tip off comedy; "hourlong episodic" points to nighttime drama; "team of investigators"—say it with me—Procedural Tone; and *Schitt's Creek*, well, you get it.)

Even if the synopsis is provided for you, read the *entire* script if it's available. If you're auditioning for a TV or film role, you may just get your scene(s). Sometimes you can get a hold of the other roles either through your agent or a casting website like Breakdown Services. If that's the case, read as many scenes as possible to find out as much as you can about the script.

WHY READING THE SCRIPT MATTERS: Here's one good example of why reading as much of the script as possible helps you make the right choices. Typically, in a romantic comedy, the two love interests start their relationship as antagonists. If an inexperienced actor only reads a scene from the beginning of the story, they quite often make the mistake of choosing a mortal enemy as a Hot Person, rather than a person with whom they have hot (volatile) chemistry and will be kissing by page 90—the formula for every good rom-com!

What type of project is it, and what is the Tone?

This is in the context of a project for a TV show or film, yet you can use the same principles if you're auditioning for the school play or doing a scene in class.

Is this a new work (TV pilot, new film) or is it a preexisting TV series or film franchise?

If it's new:

- Who is the screenwriter/playwright? Look up their past titles and find out as much about them as possible. See if there are recurring themes in their work.
- Who is the director, if applicable? Look them up as well, and see if they have a particular style of directing or a particular genre of projects in their filmography.
- How is the dialogue written—is it grounded and realistic or stylized, like melodramatic soap opera, quirky comedy, or heightened action drama? Does it have a perceivable rhythm?
- Does the title provide a clue, like *Schitt's Creek*, *Zombie Zookeepers*, or *The Pittsburgh Prosecutors*? (I made up those last two. Still waiting, Netflix.)
- Whether it's a comedy or drama, can you find an existing show to compare it to?
- Is it set in the present day or a particular historical period?
- Based on all of the above plus your previous research, what is the overall tone of the project?

If it's preexisting, or already produced:

- For a TV show: Find clips of the show on YouTube or episodes on a streaming channel like Netflix or Hulu to determine the tone. Read synopses of the series on the internet. (If it is an episodic with a Procedural Tone, determine if elements of the Steven Hill exercise are applicable.)

- For a scene in class from a film that you have not watched in its entirety: Try to find the screenplay online or a clip on YouTube to acquaint yourself with the tone, and read synopses of the film to understand the storyline.

- For a play: Read the entire play. Find the synopsis on SparkNotes or a similar website, if applicable, or summarize the plot yourself.

WHAT IS MY ROLE, AND WHAT EXERCISES CAN I USE TO START CONNECTING TO IT?

What type of role are you reading for? Starring, supporting, or costar? (Usually, a costar is a character that does not have a storyline and may be anywhere from several pages to one line.) It's usually very clear what your role is. Most of the time, your audition invitation will say the character's name or title with a brief description, like TERRY (30–40, a romantic at heart with a stubborn streak, SERIES REGULAR) or DOCTOR (30–60, works in the ER, COSTAR, 2 lines).

Class is a great dress rehearsal for your working actor career, where you'll play lead roles in scenes from TV, film, or plays. Or you might be a character supporting the lead—like a mom or best friend. Or you might be an antagonist trying to thwart the lead. Or a bank teller cashing a check for the lead. All of these parts are important and, depending on the script and/or character descriptions, have different requirements of the actor. Our job is to know how our character fits into the narrative.

When you've ascertained the type of role you'll be playing, you may already instinctively know which Act ALIVE exercises provide the best way for you to merge with your character. If not, here are some tips.

If you're reading for a starring role or series regular, you must determine what your character wants and what their journey is, aka I Need—Annie seeking love in *Bridesmaids*, T'Challa saving his people in *Black Panther*, or Rick protecting his son Carl on *The Walking Dead*. The actor in a starring role in a movie, TV show, play, or scene in class must be in touch with their I Need in order to connect to their character's I Need. You may also have a Mode of Being (T'Challa = African

King, Rick Grimes = Southern sheriff, etc.).

If you are reading for a supporting role, your character is either supporting the lead on their journey to achieve what they want, like Sam's devotion to Frodo Baggins in *Lord of the Rings*, or you might be an antagonist to the lead and are attempting to thwart their journey. Whether you're a supporter or a thwarter (that's actually a word) you must be in touch with your I Need because your character has a journey as well. A good example of an antagonist's I Need is Killmonger's in *Black Panther*—growing up orphaned in America after his father was assassinated, he strongly believes Wakanda's best chance at survival is to fight white colonialists and take a more offensive posture in world affairs.

If you are reading for a costar, your character is usually one that moves the story along and quite often can be accessed by using Mode of Being and/or Do Your Job! In *David Makes Man*, my character, Mrs. Eucliffe, represents Hurston Prep, a school that David aspires to attend. Mrs. Eucliffe speaks to David and a small group about the advantages and exclusivity of Hurston. My preparation was the Mode of Being of upper middle class, Professional Mode of Being of school administrator, High Status, along with some chosen Actions (to impress, to connect, to inspire).

Some costar roles do require connection. For example, there are many roles of grieving mothers, fathers, and other family members in medical and procedural dramas having just lost a loved one in a hospital or in a dramatic courtroom scene. You are still moving the story along; however, your character has been greatly affected by the events of the story. My role in *The Shadow Effect* is also an example of this type of character who is not central to the storyline but has been traumatically affected by the actions of the movie's lead. Any number of exercises can help you achieve this connection—your Personal Scene, Hot Person, Hot Situation, Hot Person Confrontation, Memory, and in my case, the right Actions.

ZOOMING IN

If the script's good, everything you need is in there. I just try and feel it, and do it honestly.
—Olivia Colman

Now that you have a holistic view of the project and your role in it, let's talk about breaking it down, one scene at a time, whether you have one or several. This chapter is about how each Act ALIVE exercise has the potential to bring truth, definition, and even excitement for each moment in a scene.

To give you a little perspective on how to identify the elements of your character's story, think in terms of your Personal Scene. That was told from the point of view of you in the lead role. If we were to enact several more Personal Scenes from other significant moments of your life, we would get more glimpses of your journey as a human being. Some parts of that journey were when you were the most challenged or were searching for your heart's desire (I Need). You could identify the supporting characters and villains (Hot Persons and maybe some Hot Person Confrontations), the harrowing circumstances (Hot Situations), your greatest moments of persuasion (I Believe). We'd observe your behavior at work (Do Your Job!), your party persona (Mode of Being), at home with a companion (Everyday Scene), or quietly alone (Private Moment), how you related to your past (Memory), how your nonverbal behavior changed according to your circumstances (Body Language), and what steps you took to overcome obstacles (Actions). Do you see how all of these relatable scenarios correspond to your Act ALIVE tools?

Now we are using our experiences as human beings and our gifts as actors to tell the story of a character, lifting them off the page and bringing them to life. We are illusionists—creating a world, a reality—so that anyone observing this world, either on film or on stage, believes our character exists and that our life continues, even when the credits roll or the curtain comes down.

WHAT IS MY I NEED *RIGHT NOW*?

What are you trying to accomplish in the scene, aka your I Need *right now?* Are you saving your daughter from kidnappers, convincing a jury to convict a murderer, or planning a hookup with Romeo? Assess what the scene is about, and sum up your purpose and what you need to accomplish in the scene according to your role. (For clarity, it helps to summarize the scene in one sentence with your character in third person e.g., "Sheila breaks up with her husband.") Using your I Need makes your character's objective meaningful to you. Saving your daughter is a different kind of objective than your Romeo rendezvous—and yet the I Need in both should be palpable.

Is it possible for you to simply connect to your character's I Need without consciously using your own? Of course—that may have been what drew you to the character in the first place. When you did the I Need exercise, you discovered the muscle memory of urgently needing to accomplish something that you can use for any character. That may be all *you* need.

Who are the Hot Persons in my scene(s)?

Identify the Hot Persons you are interacting with, whether you have one scene or the lead in the movie. Choosing the appropriate Hot Persons impacts your behavior, your choice of Actions, your Body Language. If your Hot Person is your antagonist, it automatically creates tension in the scene. If the Hot Person is thwarting your journey, (e.g., creating an obstacle to your progress), it forces you to make choices to overcome the obstacle. Refer to your running list of potential Hot Persons in your life that best fits your relationship in the scene.

Is there a Hot Situation?

Is there also a Hot Situation that you can relate to this scene? A Hot Situation can range from an event that is thrilling (e.g., riding a rollercoaster or watching fireworks), frustrating (e.g., misplacing your car keys or waiting in a long line), or frightening (e.g., losing your toddler at the zoo or getting in a car accident). If it applies to your scene, using a Hot Situation can put you in the same emotional place as your character in that moment.

IS THERE A HOT PERSON CONFRONTATION?

You've already read the scene and chosen the Hot Person, so if there's a confrontational moment, you have likely chosen the best Hot Person with whom to have that confrontation. Even if the opposing character in the scene does not sync up with your Hot Person in real life, you can still use the Hot Person Confrontation exercise to put yourself in the appropriate confrontational mode.

DO ANY ELEMENTS OF MY PERSONAL SCENE APPLY?

The Personal Scene was your first time using true emotional connection about a specific moment of your life. It may have been a loss, a confrontation, a moment of joy, or an epiphany. If your character is experiencing a similar moment or situation, you can use your connection from your Personal Scene and merge it with your character. It doesn't have to be apples to apples, just similar. If there are moments in the script that don't reflect your Personal Scene but are related to other moments in your life, I suggest you write a new Personal Scene and use that connection for the material.

ARE THERE ANY I BELIEVE MOMENTS, OR IS MY CHARACTER DRIVEN BY THEIR I BELIEVE?

Does your character have a moment, a scene, or a through line where they have a strongly convicted attitude or belief? The obvious example is an evangelical-style speech, but it can also be a strong point of view—even absurdly comedic. To connect to your character, revisit your I Believe and use that same connection when you rehearse the dialogue in your scene.

> BIG NOTE: Characters on a mission to accomplish change will quite often have I Believe moments. This is true for both lead/heroes and antagonists. A great example of an antagonist's I Believe is Killmonger's rousing speech about the oppressed people rising up to kill those in power in Black Panther. ("The sun will never set on the Wakandan empire.")

Are there any Memory moments?

Does your character have any Memory moments, moments of recall, a story, a reference to their history? Find a similar memory that parallels your character's, first recounting your memory out loud and now using the written dialogue to speak in your character's voice.

Are there any Everyday moments?

Without even reading your script, I can almost unequivocally say yes. Smart actors find the Everyday moments whenever they can, even in scenes that don't seem to fit that mold. Later in this section, I will give an inspiring example of how using the Everyday technique made new actors look like old pros.

Is there Subtext?

In the Everyday + Cover scene, what we *saw* was a human being attempting normal behavior, but we *sensed* there was something else going on—which in this case was a repressed confrontation— an example of subtext. This creates the tension in the scene and can work for both comedy and drama.

Many of our human transactions contain subtext. How many times have you said to a frenemy, "It's so good to see you!" when you've meant the opposite? Or "I'm doing fine" to an ex when you really mean "I miss you so bad it hurts!" Playing it cool on a first date when you're wildly attracted is subtext, as is smiling at a rude customer or feigning interest while a friend drones on.

Sometimes in our scenes we say exactly what we mean, as in a Hot Person Confrontation, I Need, or I Believe moment. However, when you read a scene, ask yourself if your character is suppressing what they actually would say in order to achieve what they want—which could range from making a sale to preserving their dignity. If you need to make a sale and the customer is a jerk, your only path to success may be to cover your real feelings.

Does my character have a Mantra?

Is there a phrase or secret statement that your character may be thinking throughout the scene? Whether it's driven by an urgent situation ("I need to get out of here!"), or a relationship ("I'm concerned about you"), a Mantra can provide an unspoken through line that informs your attitude, behavior, and actions.

Are there any Private Moments?

Is your character alone for a period of time, or perhaps involved in an activity or any other kind of Moment Before until they're engaged by another character? Or are they alone with their thoughts at the end of the scene, having an internal reaction to what just took place—aka the Final Moment? This is very important, especially in film acting when the camera is still rolling after the last words of dialogue are spoken. The director always wants to see the actor fully engaged in these nonverbal moments, just as you were in your Private Moment exercise. Incorporate the Final Moment into your work from now on, for performance and for auditions.

Do I have a Mode of Being?

The answer is usually yes, a Mode of Being can apply to any size role; even starring roles can be based on a Mode of Being. Your economic status, profession, personality type, place of birth, and subsequent speech idioms or dialect are information you are usually given—either in the character description or by your actions and dialogue in the script. If these descriptors are not spelled out, you can use the Mode of Being technique to bring more definition to the character. (Is she a busybody neighbor? Is he a stoic father figure?) You can experiment in the rehearsal process by playing with different Modes of Being. Keep in mind using You (as we discussed in the Mode of Being chapter) might be exactly what casting wants to see.

What is my Body Language?

Another important discovery to make when working on a script is your character's

Body Language. You may have already noted your Body Language by choosing your Hot Persons and your Mode of Being. You may be a high status character of a certain bearing, or low status with droopy posture. Your character's Body Language can reflect the time of day, whether the scene takes place at 5 p.m. on a dreary afternoon or 9 a.m. on a spring morning. Whatever took place before the scene could have a bearing on your Body Language—a person who's just been dumped by their significant other enters a room differently than someone who just won the lottery.

Ask yourself how your Body Language can reveal your character's subtext. If there's a possibility of covered-up attraction, a woman may *say* she's not interested in a man, but if she's twirling her hair and dangling her leg, her body is saying otherwise. Take all these factors into account in your rehearsal process.

How does Place impact me?

How does the Place, or scene setting, affect you? Are you at home, at work, in a strange hotel room? You already have information about the scene, what the situation and the Hot Person is, and what your character wants. Does the Place add another layer of tension, (e.g., an emergency room), or does it enhance your comfort and relaxation, (e.g., a scene in your kitchen with a loved one)?

Am I Doing My Job!?

If you're a costar or a principal role and are one of the characters moving the story along, you quite often are in the Professional Mode of Being, which I'm sure you are now expert at portraying. Even a starring role can be in a Professional Mode of Being. Part of the rehearsal process is doing research on this profession, the vernacular, attitude, and confidence that the role requires. If it's appropriate, you can incorporate the relaxation, weariness, and Secondary Activity that you learned in the Steven Hill exercise. Good job!

What are my Actions?

Are there any moments where choosing one Action or several brings even more focus or nuance to your scene? If your one line is "Somebody save my baby!" you might choose an Action to achieve your goal (to alarm, to plead, to exhort, to shock, etc.). Or it can be a quiet first-date scene where you choose the appropriate Actions to seal the deal (to intrigue, to tease, to tickle, to enchant, etc.).

Where does the scene start?

No, it's not a trick question. Your audition sides could begin with this line:

YOUR CHARACTER
I said I was fine.

As the line indicates, we are catching this character in mid-conversation. What that means for you is, given all of the other information in the script, you must know what the circumstances and relationships are and what was said previously, even if you write it out for your eyes only:

OTHER CHARACTER
Are you okay?

YOUR CHARACTER
I'm fine.

OTHER CHARACTER
You don't look okay. Are you sure you're okay?

YOUR CHARACTER
I said I was fine.

Obviously it's important that you stay in the tone and context of the script. Imagining the conversation preceding your first line of dialogue will allow you to begin the scene seamlessly.

Is there any opportunity for Improvisation?

You mean, when I get my audition script, can I change the dialogue and use my own words? Well, no. But besides making your acting seem unscripted and unrehearsed, your Improvisation skills can be used in an audition or even on a set.

If a scene starts with the description "BOBBY is in the den, watching his football team lose on TV" before another character enters, you could use that Hot Situation to fully realize the moment vocally: "Oh, NO! C'MON! Oh, CRAP!" before the other character enters. This is also an example of a Moment Before, it's just a little louder than the usual Private Moment.

Sometimes on a set, a director will ask you to improvise either before the actual dialogue starts or at the end of a scene. When I filmed *Lady of the Manor*, Justin Long (the writer, codirector, and star) asked Patrick Duffy and me to improvise some banter before we confronted our son, played by Ryan Phillippe. Not only did it prime us for the scenario, my improv made the final cut!

The Final Moment of a scene is, in essence, an improvised moment, whether it's quietly reflecting on what just took place or a spontaneous outburst after striking out with a potential love interest ("DAMN!"). Remember, this is just a moment—not a soliloquy—and is always at its best when it comes from a truthful, organic place.

> BIG NOTE: Adding dialogue—even in a Moment Before or Final Moment—could be risky if the project's creator demands immaculate allegiance to the script (Aaron Sorkin). However, in my experience, when used judiciously, these moments can flesh out the scene, are usually appreciated, and could be the winning factor that books you the role. When in doubt, for a self-tape audition, send in versions both with and without the improv, and if in person, go with your gut instinct. You're usually right.

REHEARSAL TIPS

For me the rehearsal period is the part I most enjoy. It's the creating of the story.
—Damian Lewis

Let me tell you what my attitude about rehearsing was when I began my <cough> acting career.

I hated it. Why? I think it was a combo platter of laziness fueled with a healthy dose of fear. My fear of failure was so paralyzing that I dreaded those first awkward steps of trial and error, which is typical of the initial rehearsal process. So, I avoided it whenever possible. And—surprise—I rarely booked jobs.

Let me save you years on the unemployment line by giving you the hard truth right now. When you start to work on a new script, chances are, your first attempts are going to suck, especially if you're new at this. (You think you're the only one? I've been on sets with stars who struggle in rehearsal. Everyone does. You're in good company!)

Don't expect your performance to spring from your loins fully formed—you must put in the sweat equity! In this business, there are many things out of your control, but your work ethic is one main area where you do have control. As NYC acting coach Matt Newton says, "Be the hardest-working actor in the room." That's the only way you can achieve success.

You have a great advantage, having been conditioned by those forty-four exercises plus improvisation and the information in this chapter up to now. Roll up your sleeves, experiment with all of it, and most importantly, remember the joy of what you're doing! You're not chained to a desk with a boring job; you are living the life that most people dream of. Rehearsal is an exciting process—and a magical performance is the potential end result.

Repetition

The rehearsal process can be frustrating, especially if it takes several attempts to get to the truthful core of a scene. Finding those Aha! moments requires experimentation, trying different Hot Persons to find the strongest connection, adding elements of the other Act ALIVE exercises, keeping the ones that work, throwing away the ones that don't. How do you know what works? You'll know it in your gut, and if you're taping your rehearsal takes, the camera will tell you.

During this process, you should rehearse your scene multiple times. When I was younger, I deluded myself into thinking that a scene would be fresher the less I rehearsed it. Nothing could be further from the truth. If anything, a scene becomes fresher the *more* you work on it. Not only will you discover new moments with every pass of the scene, but your lines will start to become second nature and in your bones. There's nothing worse than line uncertainty for an actor, and nervousness from an audition compounds the problem. So, use your rehearsals, your bath or shower time, jogging time, driving time, and any other time to run your lines until you could perform them riding a roller coaster while juggling firecrackers.

Listening and Responding

Quite often, your character is either driving the action, responding to the other characters, or both. After going through the suggestions we've covered so far in Part Four, start reading the script out loud with another actor. (Or a saintly volunteer, in my case my husband. If you don't have a partner available to read with you, many of my students use line-learning apps, like Scene Study or Memy.)

Pay more attention to the other character's dialogue—and LISTEN. The lines or actions that you're responding to are as important as your lines and actions. In this rehearsal process, make discoveries about how your character spontaneously responds to each moment (otherwise known as a Beat, as I had mentioned in Key Terms and the Actions chapter) and how they move forward to achieve what they want. Remember, you—the actor—know the story and dialogue, but your character *does not*. Approach the start of each scene as if you don't know the outcome. That is the key to an irresistible performance.

Memorization

Memorizing lines can be a stumbling block for some actors. Some are naturally better at it than others, but overall, it's a muscle that must be worked, like any other muscle. If you don't work it, it atrophies. Here are some of my favorite tips that hopefully will help you find your own technique. You'll notice some points made earlier in Part Four, because the memorization process starts when you first pick up your script.

- Know the story. Most actors freak out when they first get the script, especially if it's lengthy or has big chunks of dialogue, and rush to memorize before they even know the story they're telling. Take the necessary time to read the script several times, and summarize the story you're telling, (e.g., Karen finds love after divorce, or Rylan survives a storm on Mt. Everest).
- As you read and reread, start to make bullet points about each moment, (e.g., Julia starts the conversation, Julia shares a memory of college with her daughter, Julia offers her coffee, etc.). Memorize the order of these bullet points so you're clear about the outline.
- When you know the order of the bullet points or events of the scene, also know what your personal connection or action is for each of those bullet points. It could be a Hot Person, an I Believe, or just the Everyday action of pouring coffee. Keep it simple.
- Repetition. I said it above and am repeating it here. Speaking the dialogue out loud over and over—hundreds of times if you have to—helps to upload it to your brain.
- Write the dialogue out by hand. I find this is also helpful to lock it in.
- Also as said above, if you're LISTENING to the other characters talking to you, quite often your line is a direct response to what you just heard, (e.g., "Where are you going?" "I'm going to the store.").
- Using mnemonic devices—for example, if I have a list of things in a line of dialogue, I'll memorize the first initials, (e.g., "I saw quails, ducks, geese, and rabbits!" I'll memorize Q-D-G-R).
- If you have time before your audition, do all of this preparation right before you go to bed, and sleep on it. You'll find your subconscious will work on it during the night, and your recall will be sharper the next day.
- Once you're memorized, trust it. Go back to the tips in Listening and Responding to keep the scene fresh and spontaneous.

Overact

My new, shy actors quite often tend to implode or shrink on stage. Their voices get quiet, they rush their lines, turn their back away from the audience. One technique I use in class and encourage my students to try in rehearsal is to do several passes of the scene completely over the top, in other words, to overact. "What?" you might say. "I thought you wanted real human behavior?!" Hear me out.

Getting permission to go BIG can be the chisel that certain actors need to break out of their concrete shell. Quite often this "overacting" brings them to exactly where they need to be in performance. And if it's too exaggerated for the actual audition or performance, now that they're freed up, they can be easily pulled back to more realistic behavior.

Another reason why this is a valuable tool, even for experienced actors, is when we get nervous in an audition or our first takes on a set, we tighten up, and our diction flies out the window. Overacting and overenunciating in rehearsal is like a runner stretching before a race—it loosens up our acting muscles before the word "Action" is called.

Have the Conversation

Aaaand for my actors who have the opposite problem and are always BIG in capital letters, I have them sit down on a chair, making eye contact with the other human being, and simply say their dialogue as a conversation. Why? Because most scenes are conversations. Talk. Listen. Respond. This takes us back to that Everyday mode of human behavior that's so important, I sneaked it in here again.

Adding Comedy to Drama and Drama to Comedy

Some wise person said something to the effect of "Find the comedy in drama and the drama in comedy." This may not apply to every scene—for example, parents grieving the loss of a child—and yet whenever possible, I direct my students to find humor in the darkest scenes and find the dramatic truth in a comedy.

You may have heard the phrase "one note," where the acting and dialogue is relentlessly fraught, melodramatic, or self-pitying. This tone rarely rings true because real life doesn't work that way. I've had my biggest laughs at funerals—even at my greatest depth of sadness. Humans are always looking to overcome grief, to find the silver lining, to persevere—at least the humans we want to see on stage or screen. So, as a general note, your character must never wallow in self-pity but always try to overcome the circumstances, no matter how sad.

If appropriate, especially in a dramatic scene, look for a moment where you can add some humor or at least irony. In class, I may give an actor the direction of "doing the comedy version" of a scene—in other words, playing it for laughs. This is part of the rehearsal process—experimenting and making discoveries—and sometimes we'll find a moment or several that we keep in the final version of the scene. The resulting effect is a more three-dimensional, relatable performance.

Tempo and Pace

Speaking of comedy, almost all comedic scenes written with witty dialogue benefit from a quicker tempo. Think of *Veep*, *Gilmore Girls*, Oscar Wilde plays, slapstick comedies. When you are first working on a scene, it may be slow as you are making discoveries, but as soon as you can, speed up the dialogue and the pace of the scene. An added benefit is to perform in front of an audience—you'll begin to get a sense of the rhythm and where the laughs are. You'll also learn not to talk over (or step on) the laughs that you've worked so hard to earn.

Make a Truthful Statement

When an actor performs a new scene in class, I usually don't take extensive notes during the first run. Rather, I'm watching the scene holistically, asking myself—do I believe what I'm watching? New-student scenes usually need a lot of extensive surgery, however, my advanced students may only have an off moment here and there, like playing a sour note in a concert. Quite often, those moments are fixed simply by making a Truthful Statement. This little technique works like a charm every time.

Lines like "I'm from Mars," "I'm a drug addict," or "I hate men," may not ring true from an actor's lips because they don't believe what they're saying and they feel uncomfortable with that line. In those cases, I'll stop the scene, have them make a truthful "I" statement about themselves, and then repeat the line. When an actor states, "I'm from San Antonio," then they can find the truth in "I'm from Mars." "I'm a chocoholic" = "I'm a drug addict." "I hate roaches" = "I hate men." My actor Roland struggled with the line, "I'm the janitor of God" from *The Fisher King* until he stated, "I'm the father of two girls." After that quick adjustment, we truly believed he emptied God's wastebaskets.

In rehearsal, when you come across a moment in a script that you just can't connect to, speak your own Truthful Statement out loud, and then say the text from that same truthful connection. It's another tool you can use to add another layer of authenticity.

This is just a suggestion of how to navigate the rehearsal process with some of the Act ALIVE exercises. You will eventually find your own method (and maybe write your own book).

You've already experienced working in layers in the Everyday Cover scene, where you had two elements working at the same time—a Hot Person Confrontation that had to be covered/contained in an Everyday mode. You can apply the same principle when adding each Act ALIVE tool in your rehearsal process. Adding a new concept can do many things—it can either add another dimension of richness, or it can change the course of your scene to a new, more exciting direction.

When you read the script, one or two elements may jump out at you (Hot Person Confrontation! I Believe!). If they do, that will provide you a rich foundation upon which to build the rest of the scene. If not, try this sequence for a Leading or Supporting Role.

For the Overall Project:
1. (Know the) Story
2. (Know the) Tone

3. I Need
4. Mode of Being (which can inform your character's Body Language)
5. (If your character has an overall) I Believe

Scene by Scene (all of the above plus):
1. I Need *Right Now* (can also be Mantra)
2. Hot Person (with or without Confrontation)
3. Place
4. Hot Situation (if applicable)
5. Body Language
6. Everyday moments

TRANSFORMING A SCENE

As actors, you become an expert at starting over. Every single role brings with it an ignorance and an insecurity, and so you have to approach it with the same curiosity and humility.
—Lupita Nyong'o

Class is the working actor's gymnasium. This is where you will try things out, with various scenes from TV, movies, and plays. Sometimes you'll succeed, sometimes you'll fall on your face. But every time you get on your feet in front of other human beings in an acting class, that's progress. You always have to keep that in mind, because even though some scenes might come easily to you, others can be frustrating as hell. Like, bang your head against the wall, swear at the teacher, and storm out of class frustrating. (For the record, nobody ever stormed out of my class, but I've heard stories about others ...)

Another reason why class is so important is you learn strategies on how to approach as many types of characters and stories as possible. This book gives you tips on script analysis, but some scripts are deceptive—at face value, a scene that you at first thought was all about confrontation may really be about something else entirely. Or you may work on a script that you can't relate to at all. I believe every script is like a puzzle—for the more challenging ones, you may have to do a little more digging to find the solution.

After years of teaching both experienced and novice actors and feeling like I've seen every type of script possible, a new scene will emerge that can be a tricky nut to crack. For these trickier scenes, after a period of trial and error in class, when we found the one exercise that got the actor connected, that's all that was needed to transform the entire performance. It was thrilling to watch the lightbulb go off on the (formerly frustrated) actor's face and to watch the scene take flight. Here are some stunning examples of how a particular Act ALIVE exercise was the catalyst that transformed these scenes from blah to brilliant.

Personal Scene

The Personal Scene usually has many elements that an actor can use in scene work—at least one Hot Person, Place, and usually a very strong I Need. One of my newer actors, LuAnn, is a single mother raising a child with medical issues who needs regular doses of a drug to keep her alive. Her Personal Scene was about frantically tracking down her daughter when she lost touch with her babysitter. Her need to ascertain her daughter's safety was palpable.

A parent's love and instinct to protect a child is a rich dynamic that can provide fuel for any scene where the character has to achieve a difficult objective. LuAnn performed a scene from *If Beale Street Could Talk*, playing the lead character, Sharon, when she confronts Victoria Sanchez about falsely accusing her daughter's fiancé of rape. The first pass of the scene in class was lackluster because it lacked a sense of urgency and the need to protect her daughter—and her future husband—at all costs.

The Hot Person Confrontation is a great tool to use to win an argument or achieve catharsis, but in this instance, we needed LuAnn to dig deeper. When I reminded her of her Personal Scene, how the need to save her daughter galvanized every cell in her body—she used that same dynamic to confront the other character. As I mentioned before, there may be elements of a Personal Scene that parallel your character's—both instances were a mother going to all lengths to protect her daughter. This was LuAnn's first scene in any acting class, and the result was a terrific, believable performance.

Hot Person

The Hot Person is one of the most effective tools in the Act ALIVE arsenal. There are so many examples of how the right Hot Person makes a scene sprout wings; I'm going to share what happens if you *don't* have a Hot Person in place. Let me tell you about my student Geordie.

When Geordie started in my classes, he had no acting experience, but he had a great look and a passion to learn. After a few years, he signed with one of the top agencies in the Southeast and recently booked a nice role on a new TV series.

After his shoot, he called to tell me about his emotional roller coaster experience on set: "The first few takes, I was terrible. I almost called my agent and quit the business. The other actor in the scene (the star) looked at me like I had just rolled around in a pile of shit, and I thought I was going to be fired on the spot.

"I started sweating bullets. Then it hit me—in the scene I was giving the star fatherly advice. I needed to endow the other actor as my Hot Person—my daughter! After that, I was completely relaxed, like I am when I talk to my daughter, and turned everything around to the point that the director shook my hand after I wrapped and told me what a great job I'd done."

Sometimes even experienced actors lose sight of the basics—which are the very things that help you most. Learn from Geordie's almost-fail: Always know who the other human being in the scene is—in rehearsal, in class, in an audition, and on the set. Have a few in your Hot Person stable standing by if your first choice goes stale. And be specific. It's not good enough to describe your Hot Person as "Oh, someone I like." It must be a real human being who gets your engine going in a relationship that closely parallels the scene. It's always the first question I ask after a student does a scene in class—in order to switch out if the scene was unsuccessful or to reinforce if the scene soared.

Hot Person Confrontation

The more scenes you tackle, the more you'll recognize moments of the Hot Person Confrontation—when your character is using their power of anger to change behavior, extract an apology, achieve catharsis, or simply win an argument.

We just worked on a scene from *The West Wing*, "The Women of Qumar," Season 3, Episode 8. In the scene, the characters C. J. and Nancy are fighting about the policy to sell arms to the fictional country of Qumar; C. J. arguing against because of their mistreatment of women and Nancy arguing that they cannot alienate an ally and that C. J. has to come to terms with reality.

The first pass of the scene came across as a polite disagreement, rather than a high-stakes heated debate. As we've seen in our current political climate, people become attached to their ideological opinions, and arguments get personal. The actors used their I Believe as a foundation—which was correct—but they needed to take it to the next level of a Hot Person Confrontation to get their point across and win! After the two actors incorporated that element, sparks flew and elevated their performance.

Then there was a scene from *Guess Who*—a romantic comedy about a Black woman (Theresa) marrying a white man (Simon) and the tensions that ensued during their wedding preparations. The couple have an argument ending with Theresa breaking off the engagement. Does this scenario ring a bell? The break-up scene is a trope in almost every romantic comedy—the two lovers clashing because they're not getting what they want from each other. It's also a test: prove to me that you love me enough to change your behavior and be my man (or woman)!

At first, the two actors tiptoed through this confrontation—mistakenly thinking that two people in love would not go after each other. Nothing could be further from the truth! As any married person would tell you, the closer the relationship and the deeper the love, the harder the heads butt. When the two actors reframed the scene, using a beloved Hot Person whose behavior had hurt them and the Confrontation to change that behavior, it was like watching a completely different scene.

I Believe

By now, it should be clear what an I Believe moment is—a character deeply rooted in their belief system using the power of their belief to galvanize, persuade, inspire, advocate for change, and/or win. These moments are quite often big speeches in movies or TV.

But I Believe can also be used to help you dive into your character's point of view—even if it's ridiculous. One of the best examples of this happened in class when Marnie brought in a scene from *Horrible Bosses*, thinking it would be a good stretching exercise to play Bobby Pellit, one of the aforementioned bosses. For those of you who haven't seen the movie, Bobby is a coke-snorting, entitled, hateful misanthrope who's inherited the family business after his father's death and is now making longtime employee Kurt miserable. One of his first directives taking over was to "trim the fat"—which literally meant firing the fat people because they made him sad.

Marnie was struggling to find the character, and her attempts to sound convicted ("You either fire the fatty or the cripple, or I fire both of them") landed flatly. I directed her to drop the script and revisit her I Believe, which got her fired up. In the next pass with her connection to her I Believe, the scene was now much funnier because she believed 100 percent—through her character—that her money should not go to "support monsters." This helped her scene partner find more comedic moments—all he had to do was listen and react to the absurd things coming out of Marnie's mouth!

It's important to note that being connected to your I Believe isn't about adding volume. Marnie didn't get louder—it was her absolute conviction in everything she was saying that got big laughs.

I Need

Especially for lead roles, you should always be aware of your I Need—what you need to accomplish in your journey from page 1 to page 120. If your scene contains a crisis or breaking point where all is lost and your I Need is not being fulfilled, that provides a deep well for your personal connection.

It should be clear how to find your I Need in a drama from all of the previous examples. What actors forget is how crucial I Need is in comedy.

A classic example is this scene from Shakespeare's *Romeo and Juliet.* Even though Romeo and Juliet is classified as one of Shakespeare's tragedies, there are some comic scenes like the following one from Act 2, Scene 5—Juliet anxiously awaiting news of Romeo from her Nurse.

JULIET

Now, good sweet Nurse—O Lord, why look'st thou sad?
Though news be sad, yet tell them merrily.
If good, thou shamest the music of sweet news
By playing it to me with so sour a face.

NURSE
I am aweary. Give me leave awhile.

Fie, how my bones ache! What a jaunt have I!

JULIET

I would thou hadst my bones and I thy news.
Nay, come, I pray thee, speak. Good, good Nurse, speak.

NURSE

Jesu, what haste! Can you not stay awhile?
Do you not see that I am out of breath?

JULIET

How art thou out of breath when thou hast breath
To say to me that thou art out of breath?
The excuse that thou dost make in this delay
Is longer than the tale thou dost excuse.
Is thy news good, or bad? Answer to that.
Say either, and I'll stay the circumstance.
Let me be satisfied. Is 't good or bad?

Lovesick Juliet is unhinged with desire—exacerbated by the Nurse's playful side-stepping of her questions. It's easy for an actor to get caught up in the Shakespearean language and forget that it is a road map to one of our most basic desires and an emotion we've all hopefully experienced at least once—primal, lusty love!

At the time, my student Layla, playing Juliet, was dating someone whom she desperately wanted to marry. When she did the I Need exercise, she connected to her Need for a committed relationship. We jumped right from the exercise back to the scene, now merging her burning need with Juliet's teenage tantrum, to make the scene erupt with passion!

Everyday Scene

The takeaway from the Everyday Scene exercise is for you to have muscle memory of your most natural behavior. In the exercise, you have no agenda—just going about your daily routine.

You may have a moment in a movie where that's appropriate—natural behavior of your character living their life. However, you can use the principles of the Everyday Scene to make any scene much more authentic. My favorite example of this was a scene in class from *Gladiator* between Proximo and Maximus, aka the Gladiator.

In the storyline, wealthy Proximo has purchased the enslaved gladiator Maximus and becomes his mentor. Maximus is visiting Proximo at his home, where Proximo explains to him how he'll win his freedom. The style of acting in the movie has an epic, classical tone, however for my new student Theo (playing Proximo), that translated into a stiff performance, which we had to solve.

Theo brought props, and I had him set up a table like a banquet, weighed down with wine, goblets, fruit, and other food. He was then instructed to forget the script and invite the other actor in, as if the two of them were going to share brunch—Everyday Scene-style. While he improvised idle chitchat, he nibbled on a grape, took a sip of wine from his goblet, thumbed through a book—in other words, just being his natural self.

Now returning to the dialogue but in this more relaxed mode, the first line, "What do you want? Hm? Girl, boy?" rather than sounding like bad Shakespeare was as casual as, "Would you like some coffee?" Theo was now loose, his body relaxed, he looked like a human being again.

Even though the tone of this scene takes place in ancient times, we must never forget to bring as much humanity to the characters and dialogue as possible. Finding the Everyday-ness in a gladiator costume was an epiphany for the entire class.

Everyday + Cover

One of my favorite examples of using the Everyday + Cover exercise is in the beginning of a scene from *Dolores Claiborne.* Dolores's daughter Selena enters, bringing her a list of attorneys to help with her legal woes. The scene devolves into a confrontation, exposing the deep, years-long rift between mother and daughter. We've done this scene with different actors many times in my studio, and usually in the first take, each actor playing Selena walks in with guns blazing, theatrically presenting the papers. That's a common mistake actors make, sometimes called "playing the end of the scene," in other words, anticipating the confrontation before it happens.

To avoid that mistake, think of what we do in real life. We tend to squelch these moments of tension, normalizing a tense situation. When Gail, playing Selena, was redirected to apply the Everyday + Cover to that opening moment—covering her feelings while fumbling through her briefcase for the papers and other Everyday activities—we not only recognized real human behavior but also the pressure-cooker effect of holding back her anger. When the eventual confrontation happened, it was more truthful and even more devastating.

Body Language

I've given examples of how Body Language helps you tell the story of your character—your posture, how you enter a room, how you sit. Your Body Language can also fuse an emotional connection with your character. Here are some recent compelling examples from class.

My student Ilsa brought in a scene from *Sons of Anarchy*, where she played Tara, the wife of Sons of Anarchy gang leader Jax. Tara has tried to flee from Jax with their two sons, but he's discovered them in a park two cities away. At the beginning of the scene, she's sitting on a bench watching her boys play. He approaches from behind, startling her to jump out of her seat.

In this moment, there was no dialogue, so Ilsa did what most actors do: she shrieked and popped out her eyes. It looked more vaudevillian than dramatic. We had to explore how a human being would behave nonverbally in these circumstances.

Tara is a mother whose first instinct is to protect her children. She's now facing her husband—an unpredictable and dangerous adversary. I suggested that Ilsa have the image of facing a cobra, ready to strike, and to internally consider her options of escaping with her kids—Plan A, Plan B, Plan C, and so on. We watched the options play out on her face in real time—a woman who was not giving up but actively engaged in survival. It was like watching a cornered animal whose next move was unpredictable. The effect was mesmerizing.

Here's an example of how Body Language can help find a character's emotional core. We just did a scene in class from *Outlander*, the time-travel drama set in eighteenth-century Scotland that puts its characters through hell almost every episode. In this particular scene, Jamie has returned from the Bastille (jail) to be reunited with his wife, Claire, having just suffered through the birth of a stillborn child. Claire is also furious with Jamie for dueling with an adversarial character, Randall, disobeying her wishes. I know—it's a lot.

My actors were still in the discovery stage, and my student Lincoln, playing Jamie, was struggling to find the emotional center of a broken man. None of his real-life experiences even came close to these tragic events. We reexamined the given circumstances of the script. Here's a man who has been imprisoned, raped, beaten, lost a child, and is in danger of losing the woman he loves. Think of people who have lost everything. Quite often, as a coping mechanism, they become numb in order to survive.

I suggested that Lincoln incorporate that numbness in the scene to discover where it would take him. In the next take of the scene, he entered the room, his body bowed and his eyes softly unfocused. He sank into a chair and spoke in a hollow tone. Reflexively, his eyes welled up. The effect was heartbreaking, and although I'm not an easy crier in class, I had to fight the tears.

Mode of Being

By now you recognize Mode of Being as not only being useful for storytelling by quickly recognizing a character archetype—but also as a way for you to embrace a role by focusing on physical, cultural, and behavioral attributes. Many of your first professional bookings will likely be a supporting Mode of Being–type role.

Starring roles can also have a Mode of Being. Some lead characters have a distinctive regional dialect stamp, like those in *The Godfather*, *Goodfellas*, *The Departed*, *Good Will Hunting*, *Friday Night Lights*, and *Fargo*, to name a few. There are sci-fi roles that conjure up an AI Mode of Being like Ava in *Ex Machina* or Mia in *Humans*. Fantasy Modes of Being roles like the characters in *The Hobbit*, superhero Modes of Being in the Marvel movie franchise or the TV series *The Boys*, teenage mean girl Modes of Being in *Mean Girls*, teenage nerd Modes of Being in *Superbad*, stoner Modes of Being in *Pineapple Express*, sales hustle Modes of Being in *Glengarry Glen Ross*, zombie Modes of Being in *The Walking Dead*. Point being—any size role can have a Mode of Being. The sooner you recognize this, the better you'll be able to bring the role to life.

I mentioned all of the above titles because many times in my acting studio, we've done a scene with one of these starring roles, and the actor usually gets the strongest connection just by committing to the Mode of Being. My student Jasper wanted to challenge himself by performing a scene from *The Birdcage*—playing Armand, the drag star of his partner's South Beach club. Jasper is straight and has never performed in drag. Even more daunting was Armand's given personality—he is high-strung and flamboyant, whereas Jasper is soft spoken and self-effacing.

The key was for Jasper to find not only an "out there" Mode of Being—but we wanted to keep it out of the cartoony stereotype. I had him go back in his life and embody the most flamboyant woman he's ever known—mimicking her voice, mannerisms, and attitude. Then he worked on the Mode of Being of extreme nervousness, which he manifested physically by quick breathing—soon his hands began to shake. Finally, we had to find a walk, but rather than focusing on "gay," we tried a rapid pace (to go along with the nervousness) and tight pants. (Armand is very vain!) We kept layering on a new mannerism, all the while keeping it as organic as possible. Sometimes going through a series of Modes of Being helps an actor find the sweet spot of a character and in turn a successful performance.

> BIG NOTE: For many Modes of Being, wearing the right wardrobe helps you drop into the character!

Place

In the Place chapter, I invited you to picture different environments and notice your emotional reaction to each. Some scenes occur in settings that can affect you deeply before a word is spoken: a morgue, a witness stand, prison, a church wedding.

In class, we did a scene from the science-fiction horror film *Annihilation*—when the character Lena has been abducted during her husband's medical emergency and wakes up in a secret facility. It was difficult for my student Bea to find an emotional connection to the confusion and terror of waking up in a strange place. I walked her through a few scenarios that might be more meaningful to her: What if upon returning home from work, she discovered her house and everything in it, pets, roommates, etc. was gone? Or what if this Place represented a deep-rooted fear, like claustrophobia (imagine being in tight quarters with no air) or fear of spiders (imagine spiders crawling on the walls). In this type of eerie sci-fi scenario, we always try to find a Place, real or imagined, that conjures up the greatest feelings of fear or dread. Don't worry about going there; when the scene's over, go back to your Beautiful Place!

My student Luigi was working on a scene from an indie film where his character was grieving the death of his sister. He was completely emotionally unconnected. I asked him if he had ever lost anyone who he loved, and as it turned out, his cousin had been killed some years back—and yet he still could not muster a connection.

I gently suggested he imagine the stage as the graveyard where his cousin was buried and "see" the gravestone with the name, date of birth and death. Using that Place finally got him to his truthful feeling of loss.

Memory

By now it should be easy for you to identify a Memory moment in a script—when a character is in a moment of recall, perhaps to get love, friendship, resolution, or catharsis. However, Memory moments can also be used to create an undertone of horror, as my student Gian discovered working on a scene from *Jaws*.

One of the most iconic monologues in film history is delivered by the character Quint, who has been tasked with catching a murderous great white shark with police Chief Brody and Matt Hooper, a visiting oceanographer. The three of them are drinking on Quint's boat at night, preparing for the battle ahead. Quint is a World War II vet and has been through the ordeal of the sinking of the USS *Indianapolis*, adrift in the water surrounded by his mates who are being eaten alive by sharks, one by one. The monologue starts: "Sometimes that shark looks right at ya. Right into your eyes. And the thing about a shark is he's got lifeless eyes. Black eyes. Like a doll's eyes ..."

This Memory not only reveals Quint's character by what he had survived, but it also served an immediate objective: asserting his alpha status over his boat mates, particularly Hooper. Were they man enough to face the same horror? Gian and I came up with a secret weapon—this was a virility contest, and his Memory was the best sex he'd ever had. The combination of the brilliant script with an almost gleeful approach at the horror it stirred made for a memorable, chilling effect. It was a terrific lesson of yet another way to use the Memory tool.

Action

As I've said before, the Action tool is effective to bring more focus or nuance to a moment. But sometimes you can create an entire performance by "Actioning," especially when you're having difficulty connecting with other Act ALIVE elements.

Case in point was a recent scene from *American Hustle*, the confrontation scene between Edith and Sydney in the casino powder room. My actors—gentle, lovely ladies—were struggling to find Hot Persons or any situation in their life that they could relate to for this nasty battle between two very complicated women. The script demands rage and recrimination. So, we identified Actions for each line, (e.g., to confront, to push back, to mimic, to destroy, to wound, to taunt), and the directive was—commit 1,000 percent! By the way, note that many of these Actions are figurative. The actors didn't make physical contact until the infamous kiss at the end.

Sometimes Actioning the beginning of the scene may be all you need to carry you through to the end, or if not you can Action every sentence or beat of the entire scene. Remember in a fight like this, both parties want to win by vanquishing the other antagonist. You may be a kind person in real life (good for you), but when a scene requires emotional gladiating, you must choose strong attack-based verbs and dive in with your entire being!

MULTIPLE ELEMENTS

When you're telling a story, I think you should tell it to its fullest, with reckless abandon and absolutely let it be what it is.
—Kate Winslet

I've given examples of how each of the Act ALIVE elements brings a scene to life. Here's one of my favorite examples of how using multiple tools yielded stellar results in this scene from *Hope Floats*. As we added each layer in class, my actors not only made more truthful discoveries about their characters, but the scene got funnier with each take. Why? *The biggest laughs always come from truth.*

This action takes place between Birdee, the former prom queen who has returned to her small hometown in Texas (after being humiliated on national TV by the confession of her best friend's affair with her husband), and Dot, who runs the local employment agency. Birdee is broke and now must beg Dot for a job, unaware that Dot is also a former classmate whom she used to tease.

DOT
Birdee! Come on in.
(To receptionist) No calls, Deborah.
(To Birdee) Hi.

BIRDEE
Hi.

DOT
I didn't keep you too long?

BIRDEE
Oh no, it's fine, thank you.
You look beautiful.

DOT
Same ole Birdee.

BIRDEE
Same ole Dot.

DOT
Heh heh. You have no idea who I am, do you?

BIRDEE
No sorry, I don't.

DOT
It's all right. When I knew you, I was about 5 inches shorter and about 70 pounds heavier. We didn't exactly eat at the same lunch table.

BIRDEE
Polka Dot? Is that right?

DOT
Yeah. Ha, ha. Nobody's called me that in a long time.

BIRDEE
Oh my God! You look fantastic!

DOT
Thank you.

BIRDEE
You're welcome.

DOT
Have a seat.

BIRDEE
Oh my God, I mean it's remarkable.

DOT
Was I really that terrible before, Birdie?

BIRDEE
Oh no no no—I just meant that …

DOT
Yeah, well, I know what you meant. People change. We get better as we get older.

BIRDEE
Yeah.

DOT
Gosh, you look exactly the same.

BIRDEE
Well, no actually, I—

DOT
Oh, I know. I heard about you and Bill.

BIRDEE
Yeah.

DOT
Yeah. He was always the ladies' man.
You all right?

BIRDEE
Oh, I'm fine, I'm fine.
You know, so much of that is staged
for TV. It's for ratings and …

DOT
Yeah. So you need a job?
What sort of work have you been doing?

BIRDEE
Um, housework. Bill worked and he didn't
want — We have a daughter.
So, I took care of her.

DOT
Okay. How fast do you type?

BIRDEE
Don't type.

DOT
Okay. Computer skills?

BIRDEE
Don't compute.

DOT
Oh, goodness.
You're gonna have to give me some sort
of idea what you're looking for here …
because I'm not likely
to find a listing for prom queen.

BIRDEE
Well, um … I used to take pictures.
I was good at that.
So maybe I could get a job
at the newspaper … or
Jackson's Portrait Studio.

DOT
It's closed down,
and the newspaper is not hiring.
I can tell you that right now.

BIRDEE
Oh, okay, okay.

DOT
So …

BIRDEE
Dot, I would really like a job.
One that I could
like myself for … even if it's just
for a little while.

DOT
Birdie …

BIRDEE
Dot … I don't know how I treated you
in high school.
I'm guessing it was pretty bad … seeing
how you're hell-bent on
putting me in my place right now.
And that's okay.
Just—Just put me in a job too.
I would really be grateful.

DOT
Well …

Shoot some pictures over the weekend.

BIRDEE
Okay, great.

DOT
I'll look them over.

BIRDEE
Great.

DOT
I'll do what I can.

BIRDEE
Thank you, thank you.

This scene is richly written, unveiling the history between two women where years later the tables have clearly turned. And yet in class, it was just blah. When we took the scene apart, we realized how much juicy material there was to work with—and we had fun watching the transformation of the actors with each added tool, which we added one at a time with each new take. By the last take, the scene was fully realized and camera-ready!

Tone—By reading the synopsis (heroine goes back to her small town and romance develops with an old friend) and the dialogue, cleverly written for laughs—this is clearly a romantic comedy (biggest clue: *romance develops with an old friend*). The fact that Birdee teased Dot back in high school is hurtful, but rather than a straightforward confrontation that would happen in a drama, Dot uses that as leverage to watch her former rival squirm and even throw in some good snarky digs: "I'm not likely to find a listing for a prom queen." The result is a comedic scene perfectly suited for a romantic comedy (aka rom-com).

Hot Person—When I asked my actor Beverly playing Birdee who her Hot Person was, she gave a vague answer to the effect of, "Some girl I used to know in high school." That's not good enough. The key to this scene is for the actor to choose a human whom they had previously mistreated and must make amends to. The behavior this Hot Person evokes is exacerbated by Birdee's I Need (see below).

For Valerie who played Dot—she must find the Hot Person who had formerly mistreated her and whom she would love to see squirm, which plays out beautifully in the scene. Who can't relate to that?

I Need— Birdee has a very strong I Need—she has lost her husband, is broke and has a daughter to support. She also must get her dignity and self-esteem back after having been so publicly humiliated. Because this is a romantic comedy, the overall I Need for the lead character in any romantic comedy is to find love. However, the overwhelming I Need in this scene is for her to persuade Dot to say yes to her need of a job. Love is her overall Need; a job is her I Need *Right Now*.

The actor playing Dot can also find an I Need—of giving Birdee a taste of her own medicine. Revenge is a powerful I Need!

Personal Scene— If the actor playing Birdee has a Personal Scene that relates to her I Need—betrayal by a spouse or friend, needing money, taking care of a child, being humiliated—these can all enrich her connection to the scene. Same for the actor playing Dot—confronting a former tormentor who is now struggling and needs her help.

Mode of Being — This takes place in a small town in Texas. Do you think Dot's character would embody all of those Texas small town-isms? You bet she would. She might have a Texas dialect, hairstyle, and mannerisms of that region.

Birdee's character can also incorporate elements of Mode of Being. She at one time was prom queen—although she is past her glory days, at one time she was the pretty, popular girl. Even during the most uncomfortable moments when Dot is twisting the knife, she attempts—unsuccessfully—to use her prom queen charm to win Dot over.

Place— There are elements of Place for both actors. For Dot, this place is her office and she is queen of all she surveys. The actor playing Dot must have an image of a place where she is boss—even if it's her private corner at the local coffee shop.

For Birdee—she is a fish out of water in a smaller and greater sense. In the smaller sense, she is in an unfamiliar office where she must now bow and scrape for survival. In a greater sense, just going back to her hometown where she now feels out of place impacts her inner life.

Body Language—All of the above impacts both characters' Body Language. Dot's is self-assured, in her comfy office chair behind her well-appointed desk. Dot is now the head of this employment agency, so she has high status not only in general, but also very much so relative to Birdee.

Birdee, on the other hand, is a bit more tentative, especially entering at the top of the scene. She wants to make a good impression because of what's at stake. Then when she finds out that the person she so badly wanted to impress is a former target, she must have body language cues of appeasement to save this disastrous meeting.

Everyday Scene plus *Secondary Activity*—There are opportunities for Dot to incorporate Everyday (Scene) behavior and Secondary Activity—she could be organizing papers on her desk when Birdee walks in, perhaps doodling or picking lint off her sweater at various moments. It also adds to the squirm factor that she has other more important things to do than give Birdee her full attention, which is a wonderful tool to use in this scene and any other scene for an actor exerting power.

Memory—There are Memory moments dotted (no pun intended) throughout the scene. When Dot says:

```
"When I knew you, I was about 5 inches
shorter and about 70 pounds heavier. We
didn't exactly eat at the same lunch
table."
```

she says it wryly, however it's based on a painful memory. The actor needs to use a similar Memory moment from their high school years (not a difficult thing for most of us to do).

Birdee has some Memory moments—like mentioning Bill working and even cutting herself off ("He didn't want ..."), which could signify a past argument or regret. The actor playing Birdee needs to internally fill in that moment for it to resonate with them.

Subtext— For these types of female vs. female scenes, more often than not there is always subtext, and therein lies the comedy. If this were a melodrama, Dot might openly confront Birdee and throw her out of her office, ending with Birdee collapsing in tears. But in a comedy, we cover all of that up with a smile hiding the daggers: "Heh heh, you have no idea who I am, do you?" Birdee also covers in the beginning—pretending she knows Dot: "You look beautiful!" We laugh when we recognize that behavior because that's what we do in polite society—and it's even more exaggerated in a rom-com.

***

Do you see how much richness you can mine from what is seemingly a simple scene? By adding each of these layers in class, we witnessed the building of a scene moment by moment.

When do you know when your scene work is complete? Ah, that's a question for the ages. If this were a Broadway show in its eleventh month, would the actors still be making discoveries? To keep their work fresh and alive, they absolutely should. And even though a scene on TV or film seems like a final product, that scene was the result of rehearsal, trial and error, and multiple takes. What you see on screen is a subjective choice by the director and editor, but there could be other equally wonderful versions on the cutting room floor.

Rid your vocabulary of the word "perfection"—acting is an ongoing process where perfection does not exist. Our goal is truth, spontaneity, and connection, using the best version of ourselves to tell the story of our character. If we achieve that and affect our audience, we've done our job. Now go forth, my working actor, and do your job with infinite joy!

EPILOGUE

You're a human being. Now act like one!
—Andi Matheny

This book has been a labor of love. Little did I know at the onset how much labor there would be, but every time I felt overwhelmed, I thought of a struggling actor picking up this book and using the information to transform their life. That always gave me the burst of energy I needed to bring it across the finish line while undergoing another transitional period in my highly nonlinear life journey.

In March 2021, my husband and I made the decision to move out of Florida and start a new chapter in our lives. Leaving my studio and all of my wonderful students was bittersweet, and yet in this day and age, with online meeting apps and airline tickets, we are never far away from one another. And nothing warms my heart more than to get the text or email: "I just booked a job!" In the last two weeks, I've heard from no less than a dozen students who are on sets ranging from a national commercial to a Hallmark Channel movie to a movie playing opposite Ralph Fiennes. These were all my "kids," who started with no previous professional experience, and now their success makes me burst with pride.

No matter where you live or what your experience is, if you have passion and a work ethic, you can realize your dreams. I've witnessed that firsthand, so I know it's true. This book was an excellent beginning; now it's time for you to put it into practice. Don't wait for anyone to give you permission—just follow your heart and start taking the steps now.

You are the star of your own life. I wish you a happy ending.

ABOUT THE AUTHOR

Andi Matheny has done almost every type of entertainment industry job while remaining fully clothed. (Well, there *was* that nudist stint on *Monk*. Never mind.) While in Los Angeles, she starred in dozens of commercials, including a high-profile stint for Olay, and appeared in several TV series, most notably *The Mentalist*, *Zoey 101*, *The Suite Life of Zack and Cody*, *Ugly Betty*, and the aforementioned *Monk*. During her sabbatical from acting, she hosted the TV shows *Kwik Witz*, *Essentials*, *Fit Resort & Spa*, and *Friends or Lovers*. Her recent credits include the recurring role of Dr. Kelly Whitley on *The Resident*, *David Makes Man*, the Hallmark Channel movie *True Love Blooms*, *Lady of the Manor* directed by Justin and Christian Long, and the feature film *High Expectations* playing opposite Kelsey Grammer. Andi created and starred in the web series *Good Morning St. Pete!* and won the 2018 Sunscreen Film Festival award for Best Web Series as well as Best Actress at the 2018 Tampa Bay Underground Film Festival. Besides her marriage to screenwriter Tom Flynn, she considers her acting studio her greatest achievement and an ideal premise for a Lifetime movie. (Waiting for offers, y'all.)

ACKNOWLEDGMENTS

Writing a book feels very much like pushing a boulder up a hill every day for months on end. I want to give my heartfelt thanks to the people who were at my back, helping with the heave-ho.

Thanks to my early readers, Laura Brugnoni, Cynthia Crass, Lisa L. Kirchner, and Karleigh Chase LaBudde (who was one of the first members of my studio, where she also met her husband, Jamie. You're welcome). Thanks also to Elizabeth Greene, Tom Parks, and Michele Yeager for their meticulous and invaluable proofreading and feedback.

Thanks to Dr. Eric Castellucci, Chris McCray, and Buzz Van Dyke for their technical language. Thanks to Walt Belcher, Helen Keaney, and Sara Minton-Oglesby for weighing in on the Tone chapter. Thanks to the amazing improv teacher Lisa Frederickson for her generosity and to my Shakespeare expert, Jan Neuberger.

Thanks to the literary agents Cora Markowitz and Cassie Gross from the Georges Borchardt Agency, and Lori Styler from the Barbara Hogenson Agency. And big thanks to Andy Cohen from Grade A Entertainment who always returned my emails and is just a heck of a great guy.

Thank you to Charles Freericks for gracing these pages with his beautiful writing. Please buy his books and plays on Amazon, especially *Eight Miles from New York* and *Six Other Plays*.

Thanks to my theatrical agents David Arrigotti at the Daniel Hoff Agency, Dawn and George Landrum from Landrum Arts LA, and Albert Bramante from Bonafide & Emerging Artists. May every actor be lucky enough to be represented by agents who are not only great at their job, but lovely human beings.

Thanks to Jillian Kinsman-Barrett, without whom there may have never been an acting studio. Thanks to Eugenie Bondurant for being my supportive wing-woman, and her husband, Paul Wilborn, for his helpful advice in publishing this book.

Thanks to Effie Lavore for her suggestions in organizing my material, and to Joe

Pierson for his expertise in perfecting the written word.

Thank you to Amy J. Cianci and the team at St. Petersburg Press for their professional guidance, and for not laughing when I asked first-time author rookie questions.

Thanks to Jason Jones, attorney extraordinaire at Thorpe North & Western, who so patiently answered my preliminary questions about publishing. And big thanks to Martin Schwimmer, who generously shared his vast knowledge of IP, and is an innovative genius in the field of frozen molds. Don't ask.

There are no adequate words to describe my gratitude to Marc Brugnoni, who not only was the last word on font size, but who like the cavalry, swept in at the eleventh hour to design the book cover of my dreams. Anyone who likes creative genius should hand the keys to Marc and pay him millions of dollars.

And then there's my husband Tom Flynn, who never thought twice about dropping a screenplay project mid-page to fix the plumbing at the studio and who makes me laugh every day. I love you doesn't quite cover it, but it'll have to do for now.

APPENDIX

PART ONE — THE ESSENTIAL ACTOR

HOT BUTTONS

Additional Hot Person Mini-Scenes

You: Is it hot in here?
Hot Person: I'm fine.
You: You always say you're fine.

You: I think I'm done.
Hot Person: Me too.
You: So, what next?

You: Are you still here?
Hot Person: What does it look like?
You: It looks like you're still here.

You: I'm finished, was there anything else?
Hot Person: No, you can go.
You: Actually, I'm not finished.

You: There's a simple solution to this.
Hot Person: I don't think so.
You: Please don't make it complicated.

PART TWO — THE PASSIONATE ACTOR

I BELIEVE

©2011 Deedle-Dee Productions. The Office, Season 7 Episode 24 "Search Committee" written by Greg Daniels (developed for American television by) (Writer) (teleplay by); Paul Lieberstein; Ricky Gervais (based on the BBC series "The Office" created by) (teleplay by) (Writer); Stephen Merchant (based on the BBC series "The Office" created by) (teleplay by) (Writer.) All rights reserved. Source: Internet Movie Database.

Anchorman: The Legend of Ron Burgundy © 2004 written by Will Ferrell and Adam McKay. Dreamworks Pictures. All rights reserved. Source: Internet Movie Database.

Bridesmaids © 2011 written by Kristen Wiig and Annie Mumolo. Universal Pictures. All rights reserved. Source: Internet Movie Database.

Wall Street © 1987 written by Stanley Weiser and Oliver Stone. Twentieth Century Fox. All rights reserved. Source: Internet Movie Database.

Inglorious Basterds © 2009 written by Quentin Tarantino. Universal Pictures. All rights reserved. Source: Internet Movie Database.

MEMORY

Passion Fish ©1992 Written by John Sayles. Sony Pictures. All rights reserved. Source: Internet Movie Database.

The Laramie Project © 2002 written by Moisés Kaufman (play) (screenplay); Stephen Belber (play) (as Tectonic Theatre) (screenplay) (as Tectonic Theatre); Amanda Gronich (play) (as Tectonic Theatre) (screenplay) (as Tectonic Theatre); Greg Pierotti (play) (as Tectonic Theatre) (screenplay) (as Tectonic Theatre); Kelli Simpkins (play) (as Tectonic Theatre) (screenplay) (as Tectonic Theatre); Jeffrey LaHoste (play) (as Tectonic Theatre) (screenplay) (as Tectonic Theatre); John McAdams (play) (as Tectonic Theatre) (screenplay) (as Tectonic Theatre); Leigh Fondakowski (play) (as Tectonic Theatre) (screenplay) (as Tectonic Theatre); Andy Paris (play) (as Tectonic Theatre) (screenplay) (as Tectonic Theatre; Barbara Pitts (play) (as Tectonic Theatre) (screenplay) (as Tectonic Theatre); Stephen Wangh (play) (as Tectonic Theatre) (screenplay) (as Tectonic Theatre.) Home Box Office. All rights reserved. Source: Internet Movie Database.

ACTIONS

The Shadow Effect © 2017 written by Chad Law, Evan Law, George Abbott Clark (writer (screenplay)) (co-writer); Anthony Feole (screenplay) (as Tony Feole.) DV3 Productions. All rights reserved. Source: Internet Movie Database.

PART THREE — THE PRAGMATIC ACTOR

MODE OF BEING

©2007 Home Box Office, Extras, Season 1 Episode 5 "Sir Ian McKellan" written by Ricky Gervais and Stephan Merchant. All rights reserved. Source: Internet Movie Database.

BODY LANGUAGE

Pulp Fiction © 1994 written by Quentin Tarantino (stories by) and Roger Avary (stories by.) Miramax. All rights reserved. Source: Internet Movie Database.

THE STEVEN HILL EXERCISE

Steven Hill Exercise—*Law & Order* episodes with time stamps. Episode numbers are as listed on IMDb and may differ on Amazon.com. (My favorite scenes have *)

SEASON 1 — EPISODE 1 — "PRESCRIPTION FOR DEATH"

35:54 This is a short scene but epitomizes Steven Hill's brilliant Secondary Activity. As the scene opens, he's sitting at his desk twisting a piece of paper as he listens to Richard Brooks, playing Paul Robinette, lay out the details of a current case.

SEASON 1 — EPISODE 2 — "SUBTERRANEAN HOMEBOY BLUES"

34:48 Short scene where Adam visits Ben Stone in his office.

42:39* Notable for Adam's attitude in what might normally be considered a confrontation.

(This episode is also notable for featuring a young Cynthia Nixon.)

SEASON 1 — EPISODE 3 — "THE REAPER'S HELPER"

26:19** Note Steven Hill's Body Language during his dialogue and refer to the Body Language chapter. What does it say about his status? Confidence?

35:36 Short scene where Adam gets a phone call with news about a copycat killer inspired by the defendant. Note his Body Language in the scene. What does it tell you about the time of day and how he feels in that moment?

SEASON 1 — EPISODE 4 — "KISS THE GIRLS AND MAKE THEM DIE"

25:03 This is probably as heated as Adam ever gets. Notice how he handles the confrontation and how he still injects humor.

30:42 Adam and Ben discuss how the defense witness list is stacked against them. Note how Adam thinks while he talks and looks at his environment while he's processing.

39:56 Adam, Ben and Paul discuss the possibility of a plea bargain. Note even while Adam is giving a directive in the face of opposition ("Try.") he always maintains control.

SEASON 1 — EPISODE 7 — "BY HOOKER BY CROOK"

38:34 Just watch this scene. It's effortless acting. Note again by his demeanor what time of day you think this scene takes place.

SEASON 1 — EPISODE 12 — "LIFE CHOICE"

26:41** Adam, Paul and Ben are discussing an abortion case. Adam actually admits to being angry and yet he remains in his Mode of Being.

33:43* I love this scene—note how Adam is considering the problem but the actor is not overplaying.

]SEASON 1 — EPISODE 16 PT. 2 — "TORRENTS OF GREED"

6:30 Adam is discussing a case with Ben and Paul while reading a document. Notice how he multitasks and how his split focus (Walking and Chewing Gum exercise) adds dimension to the scene.

37:23* Adam tells Ben he doesn't have enough evidence to go to trial. Note that he's writing while he's speaking—his focus is split. Again, he does not lose control and yet makes his point.

SEASON 2 — EPISODE 1 — "CONFESSION"

33:31* The scene starts with Adam walking with Ben and Paul into his office. We see some uncharacteristic temper as they're discussing a suspected cop killer in a flawed case. Note his process as he thinks through a solution.

SEASON 2 — EPISODE 2 — "THE WAGES OF LOVE"

24:34 Another walking-and-talking scene with Adam, Ben, and Paul. Adam multitasks—gets messages from his secretary, reads a brief while urging them to take a deal.

29:06 Adam does business with his files and briefcase while discussing a "key" moment with Ben as he's preparing to leave.

34:34* Excellent scene with Adam recounting his first murder case to Ben and Paul. Note details—his state of mind and fatigue, memory, how he makes even moments on the phone with his secretary believable. This episode is notable because it features Jerry Orbach as Frank Lehrman, the only other character he played besides Lennie Briscoe. The *Law & Order* franchise was well known for recasting actors in different roles.

SEASON 2 — EPISODE 3 — "ARIA"

42:02 Adam, Ben and Paul are in Adam's office, talking through their theory of a mother's guilt for her daughter's death. Again, notice how the late hour and perhaps a headache affects Adam.

SEASON 2 — EPISODE 4 — "ASYLUM"

35:34 Note how Steven Hill creates a spontaneous moment when Adam is amused by a petition to appeal.

SEASON 2 — EPISODE 5 — "GOD BLESS THE CHILD"

21:52 Adam and Ben debate what charges to bring against parents whose religious convictions prevented them from getting their child medical care. Again, note the body language and headache when he anticipates an upcoming theology debate.

SEASON 2 — EPISODE 6 — "MISCONCEPTION"

38:59 Adam, Ben, and Paul debate the criminality of a despicable act committed by a couple. Note Adam's tone when he says, "Get these bastards off the street." How would you have interpreted that line on paper, and how would the Professional Mode of Being change your interpretation?

SEASON 2 — EPISODE 11 — "HIS HOUR UPON THE STAGE"

24:27 Adam is studying, we assume, a law book while admonishing Ben for making an arrest without a motive. Note how multitasking adds dimension to the scene.

SEASON 2 — EPISODE 19 — "THE FERTILE FIELDS"

33:29 As Ben and Paul are arguing details of a case, Adam is packing his suitcase, rifling through folders, and dressing to leave while holding up his end of the conversation. There seems to be a bit of urgency to his desire to leave, whether it's a matter of keeping an appointment or getting away from the two of them.

SEASON 2 — EPISODE 20 — "INTOLERANCE"

27:52 This one follows the common pattern of Ben persuading Adam to sign off on his tactics, and Adam raises objections. Even though the characters clash, Steven Hill's attitude says so much about Adam's character—his history in this job, his admiration for Ben's idealism and stubbornness, and yet his statement of the futility of not only this argument but the outcome. And most actors, especially new actors, would have made the cliché choice of petty argument.

SEASON 2 — EPISODE 21 — "SILENCE"

25:15 Adam reads letters written by a defendant and discusses the possibility of using them as blackmail evidence with Ben and Paul.

32:30 Routine scene with Adam, Ben, and Paul, but I love the sense of end-of-day fatigue as Adam loosens his collar.

39:53 A rare scene of Adam with a character other than his legal team—at lunch with the father of a victim, who also happens to be an old acquaintance.

SEASON 2 — EPISODE 22 — "THE WORKING STIFF"

27:50* Adam realizes an old law school friend may be involved in a criminal case.

34:55 Ben delivers the news to Adam that there is mounting evidence against his friend. Even though Adam is affected, he covers with a mixture of pragmatism and dark humor.

Immediately after, Adam conducts a news conference announcing the DA's intent to investigate all banks under their jurisdiction. Note Adam's Mode of Being as he fields questions from reporters.

Adam then argues with Ben and Paul about recusing their office from the case. Even though he remains the consummate professional, you can see his personal feelings come through about resolving the case.

40:58 Ben and Paul show Adam a canceled check that links his friend to pay for a hit job. You see Adam's attitude change from disbelief and disappointment to determination to bring his friend to justice.

45:52 Adam is outside the courtroom, waiting for his friend Corcoran, who has just been found guilty of paying for murder for hire. They have a brief exchange. Again you see Adam's mixture of regret and compassion for his friend and yet, he performed his duty.

IMPROVISATION

Taxi Driver ©1976 Written by Paul Schrader. Columbia Pictures. All rights reserved. Source: Internet Movie Database.

PART FOUR—THE WORKING ACTOR

ZOOMING IN

Black Panther © 2018 written by Ryan Coogler, Joe Robert Cole, Stan Lee (based on the Marvel comics by), Jack Kirby (based on the Marvel Comics by) Marvel Studios; Distributed by Walt Disney Studios Motion Pictures. All rights reserved. Source: Internet Movie Database.

TRANSFORMING A SCENE

I BELIEVE

Horrible Bosses © 2011 written by Michael Markowitz (screenplay) (story); John Francis Daley (screenplay); Jonathan Goldstein (screenplay.) New Line Cinema. All rights reserved. Source: Internet Movie Database.

EVERYDAY SCENE

Gladiator © 2000 written by David Franzoni (story) (screenplay); John Logan (screenplay); William Nicholson (screenplay.) Dreamworks Pictures. All rights reserved. Source: Internet Movie Database.

MEMORY

Jaws © 1975 written by Peter Benchley (screenplay) (based on the novel by); Carl

Gottlieb (screenplay.) Universal Pictures. Source: Internet Movie Database.

BIG NOTE: Visit www.andimathenyactingstudios.com for more resources and materials.

MARILLYN'S CHOPPED OLIVE TEA SANDWICH

Ingredients:

- One can (4.25 oz.) of chopped olives, drained
- Mayonnaise
- Thin-sliced white sandwich bread, crusts trimmed
- Butter (softened)

In a medium-sized mixing bowl, combine the can of chopped olives with enough mayonnaise to turn the mixture a light gray (about 1/4 cup.) Spread on buttered slices of the sandwich bread. Using a serrated knife, gently cut the sandwich into diagonal pieces. Enjoy with Earl Gray tea.

Made in the USA
Las Vegas, NV
14 May 2023